"You can kid the world,
but not your sister."

–Charlotte Gray

# REELS & RIVALS:
## Sisters in Silent Film

## By Jennifer Ann Redmond

Enjoy!
Jennifer Ann Redmond

Published in the USA by:
BearManor Media
P O Box 71426
Albany, Georgia 31708
www.bearmanormedia.com

ISBN: 978-1-59393-925-0

BearManor Media, Albany, Georgia
Printed in the United States of America
Book design by Robbie Adkins, www.adkinsconsult.com

# Table of Contents

# Dedication

For Mom, who always believed I would,
even when I didn't.
I love you Marmy.

# Acknowledgements

Few things in this world are as satisfying as bringing an idea to life, and I'd like to thank those who helped make this possible.

First and foremost, I am grateful to my family and friends for all of their love and support. Many thanks to: David Pierce and the Media History Digital Library, for such a wonderful (and life-saving!) resource; Donna Hill, Joan Myers, and Jessica Wahl, for keen eyes and good advice; Valerie Billingsley, for her generosity; Mary E. Finnerty-Nachbar, Robert Hagan, and Scott and Jackie Day, for sharing their families with an earnest stranger; John L. Sullivan, for the use of his wonderful piece on the Duncan Sisters; and Boyd Magers and the late Michael Fitzgerald, for allowing me to quote from their delightful interview with Fay McKenzie.

Lastly, a special thank you to Velvet the cat, who helped tremendously (mostly by sitting on my papers) but did not live to see this finished.  Miss you, Little.

# Prologue: Superstar Sisters

When the curtain first rose on motion pictures, the actors were unknown. Aside from the title, the only other information was the studio and/or the director, which frustrated a public eager to learn about their favorite faces onscreen. Eventually, the anonymous players gave way to a publicized pantheon of gods and goddesses, and a curious thing occurred: it seemed almost every lovely lady on the screen had an equally lovely sister also working in film. Hollywood took notice, casting a number of them in the "Meet My Sister" segment for the early musical extravaganza *The Show of Shows* (1929). Some burned brightly for a few years, and then vanished into obscurity; others, like the five below, not only transcended their work, but the era as a whole.

## The Talmadges

Without question, if you think "sisters" during the Roaring Twenties, you think Talmadge. Norma, born 1894, was the beautiful brunette who excelled in tragedy; Constance, born 1898, the spunky blonde nicknamed Dutch, was custom-built for comedy. Both enchanted audiences with "marvelously expressive faces, high-spirited vitality, and effortless charm."[1]

Their mother Peg—one of the greatest stage mothers of all time—decided early that her three daughters (Natalie, the middle child, was born in 1896) would be the ticket to financial security. Norma had a promising beginning at Vitagraph, as did Constance (who joined her sister later). Natalie? Not so much. (Peg's Plan B was to marry her off to Buster Keaton.)

Norma was one of the most popular actresses of the time, featured primarily in florid dramas. In *The Branded Woman* (1920), for instance, Norma fought those bent on disclosing her mother's sordid past to the man she intends to marry. Her distinctive mix of glamor and suffering was irresistible to the public, not unlike Linda Evans or Joan Collins during the *Dynasty/Dallas* craze of the

*Constance, Natalie, and Norma Talmadge.* The Photo-Play Journal, *June 1920. Photo courtesy the* Media History Digital Library.

1980s. Norma's 1916 marriage to industry colossus Joe Schenck was also a marvelous career move; under his subsequent management, her already impressive output reached top-tier status. (They divorced in 1934.)

The effervescent Dutch had her own kind of elegance, a puckish sophistication that "prefigure[d] Carole Lombard."[2] One of her most-loved characters was the spunky Mountain Girl in D.W. Griffith's *Intolerance* (1916), who's on- screen death so upset audiences that he filmed a happy ending for her and released the alternate version as *The Fall of Babylon* (1919).

Though Norma attempted two talkies, both ladies agreed their heyday was over by the coming of sound and retired shortly after, wealthy and comfortable. Norma married twice more, to actor/comedian George Jessel (1934, divorced 1939) and doctor Carvel James (1946 until her death). Constance married four times in all; her first wedding, to tobacco man John Pialoglou, was a double one with Dorothy Gish and actor James Rennie. Norma Talmadge died of a stroke on Christmas Eve of 1957. Constance Talmadge succumbed to pneumonia in 1973.

*Lillian and Dorothy Gish.* Motion Picture, *November 1914. Photo courtesy the* Media History Digital Library.

## The Gishes

Runners-up to the sisterly throne were the Gishes. Most folks recognize Lillian (born 1893), whose career lasted well into the 1980s*; Dorothy (born 1898) didn't survive as well, mainly remembered only by film buffs and scholars. Both ladies got their start

* her final film, The Whales of August, was in 1987.

at Biograph, introduced by close friend Gladys Smith, a.k.a. Mary Pickford. Lillian was the dramatic one, D.W. Griffith's muse, known for her breathtaking performances in films like *Broken Blossoms* (1919) and *Way Down East* (1920). She easily captivated audiences with a glance of her expressive eyes or wave of her delicate hands.

Dorothy was "just naturally funny"[3] and full of life. She shared her sister's large, luminous eyes, but hers twinkled with mischief. She joined her sister for dramas like *Hearts of the World* (1918) and *Orphans of the Storm* (1921), but comedies like *Turning the Tables* (1919) and *Little Miss Rebellion* (1920) were her forte.

While Lillian continued steadily in movies, TV, and stage work after the silent era ended, Dorothy's last picture was in 1946. She retired from films and focused on theater work, sporadically appearing in televised theater like NBC's *Goodyear Playhouse* until her death from pneumonia in 1968. Dorothy was married to James Rennie from 1920 until 1935. They had no children. Lillian, who forever retained her ethereal innocence, never married nor had children. She died of heart failure in 1993, eight months shy of her 100th birthday.

## The Costellos

Dolores Costello (born 1903) and her younger sister, Helene (born 1906), joined their matinee idol father Maurice at Vitagraph while still toddlers. As young women, both were in *George White's Scandals;* with Dolores' delicate beauty and Helene's knack for dancing they were quickly "discovered" and signed to Warner Bros. in 1924. Dolores wouldn't hit the big-time until noticed (and coveted) by John Barrymore, who immediately booted Priscilla Bonner for her as costar in *The Sea Beast* (1926). That same year, she was named a WAMPAS Baby Star, but it was her love story with Barrymore both on and off-screen that propelled her to stardom. The two married in 1928 and had two children: Dolores Ethel Mae, known as Dede, and actor John Drew, father to actress Drew Barrymore. After their marriage ended in 1935, Dolores—who had taken time off to raise a family—made a brief comeback, the best of which was *The Magnificent Ambersons* (1942). Her 1939 second marriage, to her former obstetrician Dr.

*Dolores and Helene Costello. Photoplay, September 1927. Photo courtesy the Media History Digital Library.*

John Vruwink, lasted until 1950. Dolores Costello died of emphysema in 1979.

Helene had minor success in films. She is best-known for starring in the first all-talking feature, *Lights of New York* (1928), and for performing alongside Dolores in 1929's *The Show of Shows*. Despite gaining WAMPAS Baby Star status in 1927, only three movies followed, the last in 1942. She was married and divorced four times, once to actor/director Lowell Sherman, and by the 1942 birth of her daughter Deirdre (with husband number four George Le Blanc), alcoholism had taken a marked toll on her health. Combined with a series of illnesses, botched medical procedures, and addiction to painkillers, it hastened her untimely death in 1957.

*Edna Flugrath, Viola Dana, and Shirley Mason.* Exhibitors Herald, October 6, 1923. *Photo courtesy the* Media History Digital Library.

## The Flugraths

Edna Flugrath. Shirley Mason. Viola Dana. Reading their names, you'd never suspect all three came from the same parents. Edna, who kept her birth name, came first in 1893; then Virginia, who as Viola Dana would be the most famous of the trio, in 1897; and finally little Leonie, who later took the name Shirley Mason, in 1901. All started as child actors on the stage, egged on by Mom's dreams of stardom. Viola and Shirley's screen debut was in *A Christmas Carol* (Edison, 1910) and Edna's was in an episode of the hit Mary Fuller serial, *What Happened to Mary* (1912).

Edna had the briefest career of the three. The bulk of her work spanned only four years, from her 1912 debut to 1916, when she followed fellow Edison player Harold Shaw to England. There, the director/actor/writer set up the London Film Company (no connection to the later Korda production company), and Edna found minor success in films like *Me and M'Pal* (1916). A budding romance begun years before blossomed into marriage while filming in South Africa, and the happy couple returned to the States in 1923, where Edna retired and opened a Hollywood beauty parlor. Shaw, who had been working as secretary for the Motion Picture Directors' Association, was killed in a head-on collision in 1926. Flugrath later remarried Halliburton Houghton, a Texas broker. Neither marriage produced children. In later years, Edna was estranged from her sisters, and the sad job of reporting her 1966 death to them fell to a stranger.

After her debut, Shirley Mason did some shorts for Edison (still billed as Leonie Flugrath); it wasn't until 1917 that things took off. Besides the lead role in *The Awakening of Ruth*, she was featured as Eve in *The Seven Deadly Sins*, an intriguing series based on stories from Ladies World magazine. Alongside George Le Guere as Adam, these five-reel features each centered on a cardinal sin: *Greed, Sloth, Pride, Envy, Wrath, Passion* (a tamer title for "lust") and *The Seventh Sin* (producers, not caring for "gluttony," based the story on selfishness).

Despite efforts to build the tantalizing themes into more than morality plays, the films did only fair business, even when reissued in a truncated two-reel format a year later. She stayed active through the 1920s, gathering over 100 films by her last credit, *Dark Skies* (1929). Some highlights were *Treasure Island* (1920) with the great Lon Chaney; *Lord Jim* (1925), based on the Conrad novel and starring Percy Marmont; and, of course, a member of the *Show of Shows* star-studded sorority. She also had a small role on television's *Lux Video Theatre* in 1956. She married director Bernard During, whom she met at Edison, at just sixteen; six years later, he was dead of typhoid fever in 1923. She married another director, Sidney Lanfield, in 1927; this marriage lasted until his death in 1972. She had no children. Shirley Mason died of cancer in 1979.

Viola Dana had the brightest and most visible career, famous enough for a cameo in *Hollywood* (1923) alongside Pickford, Chaplin, Arbuckle, and other cinema royalty. Named "Broadway's Youngest Star" after playing the lead in *Poor Little Rich Girl* (1913), the tiny (just under five feet) powerhouse quickly racked up screen credits: *Molly the Drummer Boy* (1914), *Gladiola* (1915), *Blue Jeans* (1917), and dozens more. By the early 1920s, the raven-haired beauty with the "saucy grin"[4] was the second-highest paid star at Metro. Her gregarious nature was perfect for comedy, and she shone in films such as *Merton of the Movies* and *Open All Night* (both 1924). She was close friends with several comedians, including Roscoe Arbuckle and Buster Keaton.

Like her sisters, she wasn't immune to tragedy. Her first husband, director John Collins, died in the Spanish flu pandemic of 1918. Two years later, her boyfriend, stunt pilot Ormer Locklear, was killed in a plane crash while filming *The Skywayman* (1920). She wed twice more, to football player/actor Maurice "Lefty" Flynn (1925-1928) and professional golfer Jimmy Thompson (1930-1945). She had no children. Viola waved goodbye to the industry in 1929, and though she had two small roles in the 1930s and a couple of TV guest spots in the late 1950s/early 1960s, she is best-known to modern audiences through her interview in Kevin Brownlow and David Gill's epic love letter to the silent era, *Hollywood* (1980). Her final screen appearance was in a documentary about her dear friend, *Buster Keaton:A Hard Act to Follow* (1987). She died that same year at age 90.

*Polly Ann and Loretta Young, and Sally Blane*. Modern Screen, *November 1930. Photo courtesy the* Media History Digital Library.

## The Youngs

After their parents divorced, Polly Ann (born 1908), Elizabeth (born 1910), and Gretchen Young (born 1913) moved with their mother to California, who opened a boarding house. An uncle got them into the business as child extras, even appearing in *The Sheik* (1921) with Valentino. All three temporarily left the screen to attend school at Ramona Convent, but by 1926, Polly Ann and Elizabeth—now Sally Blane—had returned to unaccredited bit roles. Gretchen was still a student when Mervyn LeRoy called the Young home. Polly Ann was needed for retakes on the Colleen Moore picture *Naughty But Nice* (1927). Polly was already busy on another film, she said, so how about using her?

Colleen Moore fell in love with the girl and helped get her a First National contract, part of which was a new name: Loretta. Shortly after, a small role in *Whip Woman* (1928) led to *Laugh Clown Laugh* (1928), as love interest to Lon Chaney. Fifteen-year-old Loretta was named a WAMPAS Baby Star in 1929, and the "promising young actress . . . different from the average bobbed-hair flapper"[5] began a legendary career that lasted through the 1950s (and briefly in the 1980s). She was married three times: a 1930 elopement with actor Grant Withers horrified her mother and was annulled a year later; producer Tom Lewis in 1940, with whom she had two children, and ended in a 1969 divorce; and costume designer Jean Louis, from 1993 until his death in 1997. An affair with Clark Gable while making *Call of the Wild* (1935) also resulted in a daughter.

Loretta Young was a rare thing. Her beauty and grace already turned heads at her debut, and despite her personal troubles, she always retained her faith and dignity. From racy pre-Codes like *Employees' Entrance* (1933) with the deliciously smarmy Warren William to holiday classics such as *The Bishop's Wife* (1947) with Cary Grant and David Niven, from her Oscar- winning performance in *The Farmer's Daughter* (1948) to her glamorous Jean Louis-gowned intros for *The Loretta Young Show* (1953-1961), she was an elegant and admired presence in movies, radio, and TV until her death from ovarian cancer in 2000.

Sally Blane never reached Loretta's level but left behind an admirable catalog. Besides being named a WAMPAS Baby Star (1929, same year as Loretta), she supported Tom Mix in several silent Westerns and landed roles in prominent 1930s films such as *Ten Cents a Dance* (1931) and *I Am A Fugitive From A Chain Gang* (1932). Her later B-level output was varied but solid, including *City Park* (Chesterfield, 1934) with Henry B. Walthall and Gwen Lee, and Crashing *Through Danger* (Excelsior, 1936) with Guinn "Big Boy" Williams. Her star was already fading when she married actor/director Norman Foster in 1937; they had a son and daughter. After 1939, work was sporadic, limited to one Spanish-language film and a few TV guest spots (including one on Loretta's show). She officially retired in 1955, and she and Foster were happily married until his death in 1976. Sally died of cancer in 1997.

Polly Ann was the most transient actress of the three, frequently unaccredited and often in Poverty Row productions. She also turned up in her share of Westerns, supporting a pre-stardom John Wayne in *The Man from Utah* (1934) and Buck Jones in *The Crimson Trail* (1935) among others. Her last role was in the Monogram thriller *The Invisible Ghost* (1941) starring Bela Lugosi. She and plumbing executive James Carter Hermann tied the knot in 1936, their marriage lasting until his death in 1981. They had one son. Polly Ann died of cancer in 1997, seven months before her sister Sally.

There was one more Young sister: Georgiana, a half-sister from their mother's second marriage. While the other three sisters occasionally appeared in each other's films, only one featured all four together: *The Story of Alexander Graham Bell* (1939), starring Don Ameche as Bell and Loretta Young as his wife. Polly Ann, Sally, and Georgiana played her sisters, of course. Georgiana barely dipped her toe into Hollywood, earning only two other unaccredited film roles besides *The Story of Alexander Graham Bell*. She married actor Ricardo Montalban in 1944; they had four children, and remained married until her death in 2007.

1 de Groat, Greta. "The Talmadge Sisters." In Jane Gaines, Radha Vatsal, and Monica Dall'Asta, eds. Women Film Pioneers Project. Center for Digital Research and Scholarship. New York, NY: Columbia University Libraries, 2013. Web. December 23, 2011. <https://wfpp.cdrs.columbia.edu/pioneer/ccp-constance-talmadge-and-norma- talmadge/>

2 Basinger, Jeanine (1999). Silent Stars. Knopf.

3 Johnson, Julian. "The Shadow Stage." Photoplay, August 1919.

4 Slide, Anthony (2002). Silent Players: A Biographical and Autobiographical Study of 100 Silent Film Actors and Actresses. The University Press of Kentucky.

5 Parrish, James Robert (1972). THE FOX GIRLS: starring 15 beautiful vixens and one adorable cub. Arlington House.


## Other Sources:

Anderson, Chuck. "The Heroines: Polly Ann Young / Sally Blane." The Old Corral, n.d. Web. Accessed August 2, 2015. < http://b-westerns.com/ladies45.htm>

Lowe, Denise (2014). An Encyclopedic Dictionary of Women in Early American Films: 1895-1930. Routledge. Lussier, Tim. "The Tragic Flugrath Sisters." Silents Are Golden, 1999. Web. Accessed August 3, 2015. http://www.silentsaregolden.com/articles/flugratharticle.html

Redmond, Jennifer Ann. "Meet My Sister: Dolores and Helene Costello." Zelda: The Magazine of the Vintage Nouveau. Fall / Winter 2014, Issue 11.

Stone, Tammy. "The Silent Collection Featuring: Constance Talmadge." Immortal Ephemera, n.d. Web. Accessed August 2, 2015.  http://www.things-and-other-stuff.com/movies/profiles/constance-talmadge.html

# Chapter 1:
# Constance and Faire Binney

*Constance (L) and Faire Binney,* Who's Who on the Screen, *1920. Photos courtesy the* Media History Digital Library.

That they were lovely was never in contention. All the magazines agreed: Constance Binney was "slight and pretty in a piquant way,"[1] with large dark eyes that possessed a "deadly aim."[2] Faire Binney was "sure some pretty girlie [w]ith her big innocent eyes and round baby mouth."[3] The brunette beauties looked so alike that only their hair told them apart; Faire had naturally wavy locks, and was the first to bob them.

Constance was born in New York City on June 28, 1896. Faire, born Frederica, arrived in Morristown, New Jersey four years later, on August 24, 1900.[4] Both young ladies were brought into a world of high standing and privilege, with father Harold and mother Gertrude from prominent New England families allegedly descended from "one of the ten thousand families that came over on the Mayflower."[5]

Originally, as happened with most of the sisters in this book, press tried to pigeonhole them into a comedy-tragedy dichotomy, not just in their preferred projects, but off screen, as well. Constance, the motherly older sister, was the very picture of "Massachusetts aristocracy," composed, noble, with a "poise of breeding" surpassing her years.[6] Faire was the firecracker, more mercurial and gregarious; interviews often had "Fritzie" crashing into the room or bounding out of it, a ball of energy. In 1919, she said, "I want to do everything there is to do, whether it pleasant or unpleasant. When I die, I want to feel that I have not missed a single pleasure, or a single pain."[7] Reviews play up that side of Faire; *Film Daily* found her perfect for the lead in *What Fools Men Are* (1922), purportedly a love story but mostly an exposé into the social life of a flapper.

Connie definitely did not inherit her serenity from her father. Harold Binney, well-known patent lawyer and eccentric, made frequent headlines around New York City: racking up speeding arrests, wrecking his yacht, even proposing to a woman he'd only known for three days (and subsequently standing her up at the altar). His irresponsible and erratic antics earned him two months in the Friends' Asylum (now Friends' Hospital), the first private psychiatric hospital in the United States In October of 1914, he was arrested for harassing his mechanic and two other men; after a ridiculous attempt to represent himself in court, the belligerent Binney was literally dragged off to spend ninety days in jail. Less than a month after the garage debacle, Harold Binney was dead of an "overdose of a drug which he had taken to relieve a headache."[8] Whether his headaches might have signaled a medical reason for his bizarre behavior is lost to time. In his will, drafted during his time in prison, he called himself an "infidel" and requested his ashes be used as mulch, where they "may prove at least of use to the shrubs and flowers."[9]

Gertrude Miles, the girls' mother, was from an affluent family, her father a member of a wholesale grocer firm. As a child, her family was accidentally poisoned by lead from a container leaching into their dessert. The entire household, excepting her father and sister Annie, fell dangerously ill, and her mother did not survive. By all accounts, even after such tragedy, she managed a normal upbringing, and married Harold in 1895.

A year later, baby Constance came along. By age four, she had her mind set on being a professional dancer. Mother, who once had similar aspirations, eagerly signed Constance up for classes taught by Isadora Duncan's sister. Daddy wasn't as thrilled; there had never been professional performers in the family and they certainly weren't going to start now! Off went Constance to private school in Paris. Incredibly bored with everything save the twice-weekly dance instruction, she rejoiced when an appendectomy sent her to London and then Scotland to recuperate with relatives. When the war began, she returned to the U.S. and attended the Westover School in Connecticut. Frederica stayed closer to home, completing her full education at a girls' school in Massachusetts.

Summers were spent at the sprawling country house in Old Lyme, a bucolic Connecticut town with a thriving artist's colony. Actress Elsie Ferguson, photographer Walker Evans, and Einstein all had vacation homes there. When Connie and Fritzie weren't lounging on the tree-ringed veranda, they were hunting, swimming, horseback riding—even learning to drive oxen. The white wood-frame house would later be christened "Gray Gables" after their mother remarried music publisher H. Willard Gray.

In Connecticut, relatives staged a charity production, with Connie part of the cast. In the audience was producer Winthrop Ames, who was so charmed that he offered her a lucrative two-year contract on the spot. She debuted in 1917's short-lived *Saturday to Monday,* but wasn't noticed until the musical comedy *Oh, Lady! Lady!,* which ran for six months in 1918. Connie danced briefly with the *Ziegfeld Follies* until a disagreement with Ziegfeld himself precipitated her departure for the comedy *39 East* in 1919. She blew the roof off the Broadhurst as Penelope Penn, a minister's daughter who takes a job as a chorus girl to pay for her brothers' education. Her natural mix of puritanical propriety and impishness helped make *39 East* a bonafide Broadway success; it ran 160 performances, and toured afterwards.

Musical theater particularly interested Fritzie. In 1918, she took lessons from famous baritone turned vocal coach Robert Hosea. His was a well-respected name in New York, and his student roster reflected it, with Grace Moore, John Barrymore, and Marilyn Miller only a few of the privileged. She unfortunately tread the boards in mostly flops, but did have one personal success with *He and She* (1920). Written by Rachel Crothers (who, incidentally, also wrote *39 East*), the modern story of a woman trying to balance career and family was a bit heavy-handed in its execution, but Alexander Woolcott called Faire "very delightful indeed."[10] Fritzie was also mentioned in *Green Book* magazine as one of three new ingénues to watch—along with Helen Hayes and Tallulah Bankhead. Not bad company!

The studios were after Connie to appear in "photoplays." She consistently refused, saying she loved the energy and response of a live audience too much to give it up. Finally, she acquiesced to producer/director Maurice Tourneur on one condition: they try out Fritzie first. "You would not want me if you saw [her]," she insisted; "she is really adorable."[11] Tourneur found them equally

*Constance (L) and Faire in* The Sporting Life. Photoplay, *March 1919. Photo courtesy the Media History Digital Library.*

*Constance and Reginald Denny reprising their 39 East roles onscreen*
Theatre *Magazine, December 1920. Photo courtesy the* Internet Archive.

enchanting and cast them both in their first picture, *Sporting Life* (1918). The film version of this old British horse-racing melodrama gained positive reviews and praised both Constance and Faire as "up to the high mark."[12]

With both Binneys debuting in the same film, the press attempted to create conflict: "Faire and Constance Binney are each hustling to beat the other to the pinnacles of stardom"[13] but who will win? How furious was their trek to the finish line, anyway? In reality, neither sister was tempted to trip the other. Columnist Arabella Boone found them "loving sisters [who] each can't resist coaching the other along."[14]   Not everyone felt the race was equal. Most folks' money was on Connie: "It was a neck-to-neck race for stardom between the two sisters—and Constance won."[15] Connie's more extensive stage experience, especially 39 East, gave her the cinematic edge. Famous Players-Lasky certainly thought so, signing Connie to a three-year contract.

Both sisters appeared in their second motion pictures for the studio with everyone's favorite profligate, John Barrymore. While making The Test of Honor (1919) with Connie, the notorious roué chased the "white dove on a black velvet cushion" around the set as the bewildered Connie replied "that's what you told my sister last week!" [16] Faire's film with Barrymore, Here Comes the Bride (1919), inspired a different analogy from Photoplay: "one of the best screen farces . . . [Binney is] a bon-bon fresher than any Huyler* ever made."[17]

Constance and Fritzie continued making names for themselves in films as the 1910s yielded to the 1920s. As Barnabetta Dreary in Erstwhile Susan (1919), a film for Famous Players-Lasky's prestigious Realart division, she was "vivacious and natural" with "genuine enthusiasm" for the Cinderella story set amongst the Pennsylvania Dutch.[18] Mary Alden played the Susan of the title. A screen version of her triumphant 39 East (1920), also starring Reginald Denny, had her "forging ahead as one of the wholesome ingénues of the screen backed by a real talent as an actress and a most likeable personality."[19] (Strangely enough, Realart did not cast Constance in their a screen version of her first stage success, Oh Lady Lady.) She figured prominently in the advertising for The Stolen Kiss (1920), a Secret Garden- like story with a dual role opposite a very young Rod la Rocque, and filmed on location in Cuba for Something Different (1920), a drama of espionage, kidnapping,

---

*
 Huyler's was a Manhattan candy company founded in 1876, famous for its slogan "Fresh Every Hour."

and love (or Stockholm Syndrome) with Crane Wilbur. Her work reached new heights in *A Bill of Divorcement* (1922), the 1932 version of which is better-known for being Katharine Hepburn's film debut. This "powerfully dramatic" story of love and sacrifice in the face of mental illness provided Connie with "the best thing she has done so far . . . a splendid performance."[20]

*Constance with Fay Compton and Malcolm Keen in* A Bill of Divorcement. Exhibitors Trade Review, *December 30, 1922. Photo courtesy the Media History Digital Library.*

Fritzie didn't fare as well on the silver sheet. *Photoplay* admitted "her film performances have not offered much opportunity so far."[21] In the peculiar drama, *Madonnas and Men* (1920), an off-the-wall drama about an ancient Roman psychic's visions of a modern love story, she was given poorly conceived comedic bits. *The Wonder Man* (also 1920), a boxing drama, put her opposite French pugilist Georges Carpentier in his inaugural role—and he was considered the better actor! Despite further work with established stars like Thomas Meighan in *Frontier of the Stars* (1921) and Kathlyn Williams in *A Man's Home* (1921), her star refused to shine. Faire was accused of being too cutesy, pouting too often, and worst of all, not photographing well. She still excelled in flapper roles and earned another after the aforementioned *Fools, Second Youth*

(1923) with Alfred Lunt. But, while her sister hitched her wagon to prestige pictures, she appeared in oddities such as *Open Your Eyes* (1919), a very special film about venereal disease. Ben Lyon was also featured in this "morbid and unpleasant"[22] production for Warner Bros; Jack Warner himself played a soldier.

*Faire with Georges Carpentier in* The Wonder Man. Cine-Mundial, *June 1920. Photo courtesy the Media History Digital Library.*

Behind the scenes, twenty-two-year-old Fritzie ditched the Charlestons and cigarette holders and chose a more genteel existence. She married David Carelton Sloane, oil man and Annapolis graduate from a prominent Philadelphia family. It was quite the whirlwind romance, David so enamored after meeting her that he proposed a week later. The wedding took place a week after that, on October 27, 1922, in Gertrude's East 62nd Street house. She appeared in six more movies, her final silent being *False Pride* (1925) with Owen Moore, then retired. The marriage ended in divorce, and by early 1927 there were rumors that Fritzie was returning to the screen. Instead, Fritzie was married again by autumn, this time to Sering D. Wilson, manager of a drywall manufacturing company. The two had three children.

Fritzie might have chosen a silver pattern, but Constance struck gold. By 1922, a movie star popularity contest at *The London Times* placed her first, above Mary Pickford. When *Motion Picture* asked about her love life, she knew what she wanted: "I think the American men are the nicest and most considerate of their womankind in the world."[23] *Variety* mentioned Connie retiring in 1923 to marry a wealthy gentleman who courted her while *The Crooked Square* toured Pittsburgh, but who he was, or whether they even got close to the altar, is anybody's guess. Connie wouldn't find her American man until 1926: Charles Edward Cotting, a banker from Boston. The wedding took place at "Gray Gables," the old country house in Old Lyme.

Both ladies seemed to be sliding back into luncheons, garden societies, and the "gay life of the wealthy smart set"[24]until 1931, when after an absence of five years (save *Sweet Little Devil* in 1924) Constance announced a return to the stage—well, a stage of sorts: she took the lead in a charity production of *Peter Pan*. Her marriage to Cotting was also heading to Neverland. By July 1932, Connie quietly divorced Cotting in Reno, citing extreme mental cruelty, then took a shortcut through the five stages of grief and remarried by September of that same year. Husband #2 was lawyer Henry Wharton Jr. of Philadelphia, the ceremony a simple one at the New York Municipal Chapel. By the time of the 1940 census, this marriage too was over.

WWII brought out the patriot in everyone, and for Constance, this meant supporting British War Relief. While fundraising in Montreal, she met a young RAF pilot, Geoffrey Leonard Cheshire (later Lord Cheshire VC), who became one of Britain's most-honored servicemen and philanthropists, founder of Cheshire Foundation Homes for the Sick (now called Leonard Cheshire Disability), but in 1941 he was a young flight lieutenant in Bomber Command. Constance was charmed by his warmth and humor, Leonard was dazzled by her bubbly beauty, and the two raced to the altar only a week after that first meeting. (They liked to do that, those Binney sisters.) Cheshire called their romance "a kind of dreamland." To his mother and father, it was more like a nightmare. Imagine the son of an eminent Oxford barrister involved with such a "vulgar little woman!" She was a washed-up actress, twice his age and twice divorced, with a display of wealth and social standing they found "gaudy." [25]

Young Cheshire took umbrage and insisted Constance had been integral to his desire to stop wasting his life and excel; indeed, it was at her urging that he wrote the first of many acclaimed books, *Bomber Pilot* (1943). His parents remained unmoved, disgusted by the woman they called "Jezebel," and so a period of estrangement followed. After the wedding, Cheshire immediately returned to England, with Connie following to his air base in York about a month later.

In August 1945, the now highly-decorated Captain Cheshire had the dubious honor of only British officer to witness the bombing of Nagasaki. No doubt this had a profound effect on his life; one of the casualties was his marriage. He moved out that September, having already begun an affair with Joan Botting, widow of fellow 617 Squadron officer Norman Botting. By November 1946, he was living with Joan and their daughter Merle, who had been born that January, and the divorce was finalized in 1950. Connie cited desertion but asserted everything was amicable: he simply wanted to live in England, and she missed the United States too deeply to remain there. She returned to her homeland and her maiden name, this third marriage being her last.

Not much was heard from Fritzie during these years. She now lived in Northeast Harbor, Maine, an exclusive area known as "Philadelphia on the rocks." She tried her hand as a playwright, penning the psychological drama *The Mad Millickens* in 1939 and the comedy *Delphiniums Are Blue* in 1945. A casting call for the latter via *The New York Times* requested "a Mischa Auer type for central comedy role of a knife-thrower." Nothing suggests either play was ever professionally produced, though at the time she needed only "a few more backers."[26]. Fritzie crept back onto movie screens in the early 1950s, doing unbilled extra work as dowagers and party guests in films like *Monkey Business* (1952) and *The Eddie Cantor Story* (1953). The bit work ended by 1955, and only two years later, on August 28, 1957, Fritzie died of pneumonia. She was 57.

*Faire around the time of* False Pride. Pictures and the Picturegoer, *October 1925. Photo courtesy the* Media History Digital Library.

After her divorce from Lord Cheshire, Connie returned to her quiet post-stardom life at Gray Gables. Her name surfaced when she received a star on the Hollywood Walk of Fame in 1960, and she emerged again in 1974 to accept the Rosemary Award, started by Tom Fulbright to remember obscure silent film actors and actresses. At some point, she moved to Whitestone in Queens, New York. She died there on November 15, 1989, at the age of 93.

[1] Mott, Martin. "Cinderella Lives Again." *Picture Play*, April 1922.

[2] *Film Fun*, September 1919.

[3] Smith, Patsy. "Among the Women." *Variety*, March 1919.

[4] "United States Census, 1920," index and images, FamilySearch (https://familyse-arch.org/pal:/MM9.1.1/MJBJ-VDH : accessed 16 January 2015), Frederica Binney in household of H Willard Grey, Manhattan Assembly District 14, New York, New York, United States; citing sheet 5A, family 75, NARA microfilm publication T625 (Washington D.C.: National Archives and Records Administration, n.d.); FHL microfilm 1,821,210.

[5] Johnson, Julian. "Plymouth Rock Chicken." *Photoplay*, September 1919.

[6] Ibid.

[7] Smalley, Henry J. "Fade-Outs." *Picture Play*, July 1919.

[8] "Wants His Ashes Scattered to Aid Plant Growth." *New York Evening Telegram*, January 28, 1915.

[9] "Wills Body to Science or Fire; 'I Die an Infidel', Says Harold O Binney." *Washington Post*, January 28, 1915.

[10] Wollcott, Alexander. "The Play." *New York Times*, February 13, 1920.

[11] "From Society to Stage – and Back Again." *Ogden Standard Examiner* [Utah], March 28, 1926.

[12] Weitzel, Edward. "Sporting Life." *The Moving Picture World*, October 3, 1918.

[13] Boone, Arabella. "A Race for Stardom." *Photoplay*, March 1919.

[14] Ibid.

[15] Boone, Arabella. "The Day of the Deb." *Photoplay*, September 1920.

[16] Peters, Margot (1990). *The House of Barrymore*. Simon & Schuster.

[17] Johnson, Julian. "The Shadow Stage." *Photoplay*, April 1919.

[18] *Film Daily*, December 7, 1919.

[19] Johnson, Julian. "The Shadow Stage." *Photoplay*, December 1920.

[20] *Film Daily*, October 15, 1922.

[21] Boone, "The Day of the Deb."

[22] *Film Daily*, July 6, 1919.

[23] Curly, Kenneth. "Constance: The Brute-Breaker." *Motion Picture*, May 1922.

[24] "From Society to Stage – and Back Again." *Ogden Standard Examiner* [Utah], March 28, 1926.

[25] Simkin, John. "Leonard Cheshire." *Spartacus Educational*, September 1997 (updated August 2014). Web. Accessed February 11, 2015. http://spartacus-educational.com/2WWcheshire.htm

[26] "New Comedy by Faire Binney." *New York Times*, July 23, 1945.

Other Sources:

Slide, Anthony (2002). *Silent Players: A Biographical and Autobiographical Study of 100 Silent Film Actors and Actresses*. The University Press of Kentucky.

"United States Census, 1920," index and images, FamilySearch (https://familysearch. org/pal:/MM9.1.1/MJBJ-VDH : accessed January 16 2015), Frederica Binney in household of H Willard Grey, Manhattan Assembly District 14, New York, New York, United States; citing sheet 5A, family 75, NARA microfilm publication T625 (Washington D.C.: National Archives and Records Administration, n.d.); FHL microfilm 1,821,210.

Mantle, Burns. "Who Killed Cock Robin?" The Green Book Magazine, October 1919.

Billboard, December 22, 1951.

The Musical Courier, 1918.

Morrison, Michael (1999). John Barrymore, Shakespearean Actor. Cambridge University Press. "Constance Binney Sues to Divorce British Hero." The Philadelphia Inquirer, June 4 1950. "Mr.s. Cotting is Bride of Henry Wharton Jr." New York Times, September 7, 1932.

"Binney, Auto Speeder, Dies." New York Times, November 23, 1914. "Poisoned by Cream Custard." New York Times, July 10, 1893.

"United States Census, 1940," index and images, FamilySearch (https://familysearch. org/pal:/MM9.1.1/KWMH-PC8 : accessed  January 16 2015), Constance Wharton, Old Lyme Town, New London, Connecticut, United States; citing enumeration district (ED) 6-96, sheet 62A, family , NARA digital publication T627 (Washington, D.C.: National Archives and Records Administration, 2012), roll 525.

"Constance Binney." Hollywood Walk of Fame. Web. Accessed September 14, 2015. http://www.walkoffame.com/constance-binney

# Chapter 2:
# Priscilla and Marjorie Bonner

*Priscilla Bonner,* Motion Picture, *October 1921, and Marjorie Bonner,* Motion Picture Classic, *March 1929. Photos courtesy the* Media History Digital Library.

From the time John Bonner and Mabel Clayton were married on December 23, 1897[1] they looked forward to starting a family. They were blessed by their first child on February 17, 1899,[2] a baby girl they named Priscilla, and about a year later welcomed Albert and Perry, twin boys.[3]

The little family had recently left Mabel's relatives in Washington, D.C. and settled in Philadelphia when the boys fell ill with gastroenteritis, a common but potentially deadly intestinal infection. Too small to fight it off effectively, five-month-old Albert succumbed in June[4]. . . and Perry, who had just made it to six months old, died three weeks later in July.[5] A heartbroken John and Mabel had another daughter in 1905, named Marjorie.[6] She was their last child.

Priscilla and Marjorie moved around a lot as kids. By 1910, they had already relocated to Michigan[7] by John's family; ten years later they made Chicago their home.[8] John changed jobs frequently, working as a journalist, agent for a fence factory, and the Army all by 1920. Priscilla fondly remembered her time in Washington, D.C. "I was raised by the same nurse who raised my mother, and she never worked for any other family in her life."[9] She returned to Washington for school, where she adored dancing. When a rep for the Orpheum Vaudeville circuit visited, looking for dance talent to entertain between moving pictures, she immediately caught his eye. "One day a man came over and said he was looking for a girl . . . he picked me!  I was just what he wanted."[10]

The Bonners put their foot down. When sixteen-year-old Priscilla wrote asking for dancing lessons, they gladly sent the money, but doing it professionally?  Definitely not happening. Priscilla gave in, but never gave up, and tried again as soon as she turned eighteen. This time, she got their blessing, on one condition: if she wasn't successful and/or financially independent in a year, she'd come home. A great deal, thought Priscilla, who gave her "solemn oath of honor."[11]

She moved out to Los Angeles, staying with friends her father knew from the Army, and found her way into motion pictures. Willowy, with no makeup and unbobbed blonde hair, she was the epitome of "the innocent, virginal heroine."[12] She teamed perfectly with Charles Ray, who specialized in nostalgic country-boy characters, in her first film, *Homer Comes Home* (Ince, 1920). That first year, she also starred opposite some other impressive names: Will Rogers, Tom Moore, and Jack Pickford, who was her favorite. "Jack was a very fine actor and he was a very, very warm personality," she said, the notorious party boy sounding more tender than treacherous. "He treated me like a little sister and protected and watched over me."[13]  She also counted Virginia Brown Faire, best known as Tinker Bell in the original film version of *Peter Pan* (1924), among her "dearest and closest friend[s]."[14]

In late May or early June, right after filming wrapped on *The Son of Wallingford* (1921), she married Allen Wynes Alexander[*].[15]

*alternately known as Alan Wyness, Allen Wynes, Allan Alexander, and a few othe versions.

*Priscilla and Tom Gallery in* The Son of Wallingford. *Exhibitors Herald, October 9, 1921. Photo courtesy the Media History Digital Library.*

Exactly what Alexander did for a living is confusing. Reports list him as a writer, director, manager, even decorated Air Force Commander. They were supposed to honeymoon for three weeks in New York, but remained in California, where Priscilla took a break from the screen to be a newlywed. Their happiness managed to last a year.

Right after their first anniversary, Alexander disappeared. "When I asked him to return," said a perplexed Priscilla, "he replied, 'Nothing doing—I'm through.'"[16] She sued for divorce that August, claiming the stress had starved her out of twenty pounds and several jobs.[17] She later withdrew, but not before questions arose involving Alexander's finances. He claimed records proved he was flat broke, but Priscilla's lawyer found him living high on the hog while secretly rerouting his paychecks to actress

Gladys Walton, for whom he was "manager." Walton, recently divorced herself and horrified to have her name in the papers again, had Alexander arrested in September for failing to account for $1,600 she'd given him to buy bonds. He argued the embezzlement charge was purely "inspired by animosity and hatred growing out of social affairs."[18] For once, he may have told the truth; the case was dismissed a month later due to insufficient evidence.[19] Didn't matter to Priscilla: by the granting of her second divorce suit in 1925[20] (and final decree in 1927[21]) the marriage had been over a long time.

Marjorie's decision to join her in Hollywood brought sunshine to this stormy time. Priscilla had it all figured out: Marjorie would live with Mom in the new bungalow she'd rented for them, and continue her education at a nearby school. Just one problem: the baby sister that stepped off the train was no longer a baby. "[S]he had on lipstick and makeup and she was smoking a cigarette." she said of the headstrong Marjorie, who had no intention of going back to school either: "'I'm through with all that . . . [y]ou're an actress, and I'm going to be an actress.'"[22]

The quality of Marjorie's work is difficult to determine today. Virtually none of her films survive, and the ones that do—The Sign of the Cross (1932), Cleopatra (1934)—offer her only in uncredited, blink-and-you'll-miss-her parts. Fan magazines blandly acknowledged her the girl "who drifted into movies soon after her sister Priscilla."[23]   Marjorie rarely got above fifth billing in features and spent most of her time in Westerns at Universal, often opposite Dynamite the Dog. It's a safe bet she wasn't doing any Gish-level emoting.

Priscilla worked in a few films during the early to mid-1920s, most notably *Shadows* (1922) with Lon Chaney, *April Showers* (1923) with Colleen Moore, and *Hold Your Breath* (1924) with the "female Harold Lloyd" Dorothy Devore. The considerable success of *Drusilla With a Million* (1925), an inheritance comedy starring Mary Carr and Kenneth Harlan, got Priscilla enough attention to usher in one of the most exhilarating (and disappointing) events of her life.

Ostensibly a screen version of *Moby Dick*, *The Sea Beast* (1925) had little in common with the Melville story aside from the whale. It was a big-ticket production for Warner Bros., with a proper A-lister playing Ahab:  John Barrymore. Barrymore personally selected Priscilla as his love interest,

Esther, the minister's daughter, but her initial joy at the opportunity soured slightly on meeting him. "He was 'Mr. Hyde' if you know what I mean. He was quite a drinker . . . I was *shocked* and deathly afraid of him."[24] She never got the chance to overcome that fear. When Dolores Costello visited the set, the impetuous Barrymore fell instantly in love and insisted she replace Priscilla as his costar. A crushed Priscilla "burst into tears and fled the room"[25] at the news. A sheepish Barrymore tried to make nice with a six-page apology letter and $500 towards lost wages, but he couldn't fix her disillusionment. "I thought I could get there with just my ability," she later mused, "but I realized I couldn't . . . [i]t was terrible. I think it did something awful to me."[26] She channeled her pain into a bold move for the time: a lawsuit against Warner Bros. for breach of contract. Courts sided with her, and she and the studio settled out of court in 1927.[27]

Priscilla appeared in four of her best films between 1925 and 1927. *The Red Kimona* (1925), a story of prostitution and white slavery, was produced and directed by Dorothy Davenport (a.k.a. Mrs. Wallace Reid), and boasted Dorothy Arzner and Adela Rogers St.

Johns among the writers. The scandalized Mrs. Bonner, a devout Episcopalian, told her daughter at the premiere, "[I]f your father had known what this film was about, he would not have permitted you to appear in it."[28] Though some critics singled Priscilla out for her "appealing characterization,"[29] most merely raised their eyebrows—and rolled their eyes. "It seems the day when 'the line' can be shown in pictures is long since passed," lamented *Variety*. "To those houses . . . who like to go in for the rather lurid stuff this looks like a bet."[30] *Photoplay* found it "[s]omething terrible . . . it started out with a good story, but somewhere the great qualities of [St. Johns and Reid's] talents got completely lost."[31] An undeterred public packed the often adults-only showings; in Kansas City it was held over due to demand.[32]

*Harry Langdon and Priscilla in* Long Pants. Picture Play, *March 1927. Photo courtesy the Media History Digital Library.*

In 1926, she costarred with Harry Langdon in the first of their two films together, *The Strong Man*. Directed by the sympathetic and intuitive Frank Capra, it was Langdon's masterpiece, what Kevin Brownlow called "one of the most perfect comedies ever made."[33] Langdon, a Belgian soldier at the front, gets letters of support from Mary Brown (Bonner) all the way from America. He falls in love with her via air mail and after the war, while in the U.S. as a strong man's assistant, sets out to find her.

He discovers his beloved just as the strong man is unable to perform—and Langdon must take his place in the show. Everyone agreed: *The Strong Man* was phenomenal. "[Langdon's] artful pantomime is a delight to watch . . . [b]y the way he is going he'll soon be in the Lloyd class."[34] By turns hilarious and warmly sentimental, Langdon was "a master of all the technique which goes under the head of comedy."[35]

Priscilla wasn't left out, critics noting her "particularly sensitive face."[36] In between her two Langdon films, Priscilla appeared in *It* (1927), based on the novel by Elinor Glyn. A romance novelist with an overblown sense of importance, Glyn explained "it"—a euphemism for magnetism and sex appeal—in typically overwrought fashion as "self-confidence and indifference to whether you are pleasing or not, and something in you that gives the impression that you are not all cold."[37] While the term existed before Glyn, she made it a trend, scrutinizing everyone and everything for "it."

Paramount wrapped the "it" fad in a weak plot about a shop girl in love with her boss, but the result was less movie and more zeitgeist: Clara Bow's Betty Lou was Everyflapper, heartrendingly vulnerable yet spicy and kinetic.

Priscilla played her friend Molly, a single mother who almost loses her baby to the authorities until Betty Lou steps in. She initially frowned at the drab, unglamorous role ("[s]he was all dressed up and looked beautiful and I was in rags"[38]) but enjoyed working with Bow. "Clara always 'gave' to me in a scene. She worked with the other actor . . . absolutely no 'star temperament.'"[39] *It* became one of Bow's most famous pictures, and made her the first official "It Girl."

*Long Pants* (1927), with the same dynamic duo of Langdon and Capra, should have been a second helping of brilliance but instead "lost its polished veneer." It was good, but not magical.

The story of a boy intoxicated by his encroaching adulthood into a romantic quagmire was funny but uneven. "It isn't one of his best pictures," reported *Motion Picture*, "[but] you go on laughing helplessly thru [sic] all the defective spots."[40] *Photoplay* liked it well enough despite "not much of a story for six long reels. . . ."[41]

Brownlow noted an argument between Capra and writer Arthur Ripley poisoned the film. After Langdon sided with Ripley and fired Capra, the director wrote a disparaging open letter, calling the baby-faced comedian "conceited" and "egotistical."[42]

Langdon, shattered by the experience, directed himself through three more pictures for First National, but the stardust had slipped away.

That same year, both sisters worked together in Columbia's "semi-tragic"[43] *Paying the Price*. They played sisters who,

*Marjorie, around the time she married Chaffee. Picture Play, January 1924. Photo courtesy the Media History Digital Library.*

ignoring their minister's warning, visit a sketchy gangsters' hang-out where they are drugged and kidnapped. Though we never find out exactly what happened, it's sufficiently terrible enough for their father to covertly kill their captor after their rescue. An innocent boy stands trial for the murder, but is one lone dis-senter away from a guilty plea. The one holdout? You guessed it: Pop. He explains why, and the compassionate jury not only votes not guilty but agrees to keep his secret. The film ends in true love (and impending marriage) between the minister and older sister. *Variety* called it "wishy-washy" and "ooz[ing] over with sweet sentiments and Godly people." As for Marjorie and Priscilla, "the two Bonner sisters look[ed] very dumb."[44]

Marjorie was eighteen when she married auto salesman and millionaire scion Jerome B. Chaffee in 1924.[45] Chaffee terrorized her with his violent alcoholism, and by 1930 they divorced.[46] Two years later, in October 1932,[47] Chaffee was dead by his own hand.

Afterwards, perhaps as closure of that chapter in her life, Mar-jorie changed the spelling of her name to Margerie.[48] She had stopped acting and was earning a living as actress Penny Single-ton's personal assistant[49] when she met author Malcolm Lowry, freshly returned to Los Angeles and at the tail end of his own marriage. It was love at first sight.

They married in December 1940, a month after his divorce was final, then moved to a decrepit fishing shack near Dollarton, Brit-ish Columbia. Margerie wrote radio scripts for the CBC, and

Lowry worked on his tour-de-force, *Under the Volcano*. The novel immortalized Margerie, not just as inspiration for Yvonne but as its superlative editor. She "frequently wrote alternative versions of specific passages," and cut down "digressive and verbose" areas. These marked-up drafts were called "Margie version[s]" and Lowry almost always rewrote according to her suggestions.[50] She also saved the only copy of *Volcano* when the shack burned down in 1944. Though the marriage was far from perfect—both drank heavily and, like her first husband, Lowry was known to be violent—they found it ideal. Margerie was, said Lowry, "the only thing holding me to life and sanity."[51]

She also wrote two mystery novels, *The Shapes That Creep* and *The Last Twist of the Knife*, both published in 1946. (A third book, *Horse in the Sky*, "a more ambitious novel"[52] about the human experience, appeared in 1947.) *Under the Volcano*, the tale of an alcoholic man's unraveling in Mexico during Day of the Dead celebrations, suffered comparisons to Charles Jackson's *The Lost Weekend* when published in 1947, but is now widely considered a singular masterwork, #11 on Modern Library's 100 Best Novels 1900-1998.[53]

Amid the triumph, alcohol was still destroying Lowry. Previous attempts at aversion therapy and even a stay at Bellevue (while in New York with his first wife) failed. Belligerent and explosive when drunk, he told a psychiatrist that things would end with him killing Margerie, or her killing him. The exhausted and creatively depleted couple returned to London in 1955, where Lowry again underwent treatment. This time was different: by August 1956 he appeared "cured of [his] alcohol-induced psychosis."[54] He and Margerie settled in Sussex, where he began writing again; both returned to drinking.

On June 26, 1957, Lowry and Margerie fought savagely after spending the evening at a pub. Lowry allegedly threatened Margerie with a broken gin bottle, sending her fleeing to the safety of a neighbor's home. She discovered his lifeless body upon her return the next morning. His death was ruled a "misadventure,"[55] an accidentally lethal combination of liquor and about twenty sleeping pills. The fact that the pills were Margerie's, as well as several inconsistencies in her story, led to suspicion almost immediately. While some to this day are convinced she had a hand in his death, all acknowledge her devotion to his legacy. She devoted a great deal of the rest of her life to editing and publishing the many unfinished projects he left behind.

She moved in with Priscilla in 1974 and they shared the apartment until a series of strokes forced Margerie into a nursing home. Margerie Bonner died on September 28, 1988,[56] and was buried in England, at the churchyard in Ripe where Malcolm Lowry was laid to rest over thirty years before.

*The Regulars, Motion Picture, November 1924. Marjorie is third from left, top row, with headband. Priscilla is first on left, seated in bottom row, with checkered dress. Photo courtesy the Media History Digital Library.*

Priscilla appeared in seven more films after *Long Pants*, none particularly memorable; she did "fairly well"[57] in a dual role for *Broadway After Midnight* (1927), and *Outcast Souls* (1928) was just "average."[58]

She married former 20th Century Fox studio doctor and well-known Hollywood figure E. Bertrand Woolfan in September 1928.[59] "He was a remarkable man, brilliant and successful,"[60] she proudly boasted years later. After one other film, *Girls Who Dare* (1929), Woolfan made it clear that was it: "[h]e said let's get married and no more work . . . I knew I couldn't have a career and him."

Priscilla never regretted her decision. "I had a very happy life with him . . . I was in love, I think I did the right thing."[61] It didn't mean she turned her back on Hollywood society. She and Margerie were still active in The Regulars, an "authentic sorority of motion picture girls"[62] formed in 1924. More than a social club a la "Our Club" or "The Thalians," members paid dues, wore pins, and devoted a great deal of time to reading and discussing literature. The clubhouse library, fittingly run by Margerie, included works by Wordsworth and Cather alongside Bernhardt and Barrymore. Margerie also enjoyed reading philosophy aloud at meetings, boring the socks off Jobyna Ralston, Sue Carol, Mary Brian, Esther Ralston, and a host of others.

Woolfan and Priscilla's marriage ended tragically in 1962, when he died in Priscilla's arms of a self-inflicted gunshot wound.[63] After Margerie's death, Priscilla moved to a Beverly Hills retirement home, where she entertained friends, gave occasional interviews, and studied one of her favorite subjects: reincarnation. Priscilla Bonner died at age 97 on February 21, 1996.[64] (No word on her current incarnation.)

[1] "District of Columbia Marriages, 1830-1921," database, FamilySearch(https://FamilySearch.org/ark:/61903/1:1:F7BG- TXG : accessed August 15 2015), John Stuart Bonner and Mabel Clayton, 23 Dec 1897; citing District Of Columbia, reference 26588; FHL microfilm 2,026,210.

[2] Date: 1996-02-21; Ancestry.com. California, Death Index, 1940-1997 [database online]. Provo, UT, USA: Ancestry.com Operations Inc, 2000.

[3] Year: 1900; Census Place: Philadelphia Ward 34, Philadelphia, Pennsylvania; Roll: 1476; Page: 7B; Enumeration District: 0896; FHL microfilm: 1241476. Ancestry.com. 1900 United States Federal Census [database on-line]. Provo, UT, USA: Ancestry. com Operations Inc, 2004.

[4] "Pennsylvania, Philadelphia City Death Certificates, 1803-1915," database with images, FamilySearch (https://FamilySearch.org/ark:/61903/1:1:JKQC-W5H : accessed August 15 2015), Albert E. Bonner, 16 Jun 1900; citing cn 27449, Philadelphia City Archives and Historical Society of Pennsylvania, Philadelphia; FHL microfilm 1,839,331.

[5] "Pennsylvania, Philadelphia City Death Certificates, 1803-1915," database with images,FamilySearch (https://FamilySearch.org/ark:/61903/1:1:JK77-Q4M : accessed August 15 2015), Perry S. Bonner, 04 Jul 1900; citing cn 344, Philadelphia City Archives and Historical Society of Pennsylvania, Philadelphia; FHL microfilm 1,839,332.

[6] Date: 1988-09-28; Ancestry.com. California, Death Index, 1940-1997 [database online]. Provo, UT, USA: Ancestry.com Operations Inc, 2000.

[7] Year: 1900; Census Place: Philadelphia Ward 34, Philadelphia, Pennsylvania; Roll: 1476; Page: 7B; Enumeration District: 0896; FHL microfilm: 1241476. Ancestry.com. 1900 United States Federal Census [database on-line]. Provo, UT, USA: Ancestry. com Operations Inc, 2004.

[8] Year: 1920; Census Place: Chicago Ward 25, Cook (Chicago), Illinois; Roll: T625_342; Page: 9B; Enumeration District: 1445; Image: 160. Ancestry.com. 1920 United States

Federal Census [database on-line]. Provo, UT, USA: Ancestry.com Operations Inc, 2010. Images reproduced by FamilySearch.

[9] Villecco, Tony (2001). *Silent Stars Speak: Interviews With Twelve Cinema Pioneers.* McFarland & Co Inc.

[10] Ibid.

[11] Ibid.

[12] Silde, Anthony (2002). *Silent Players: A Biographical and Autobiographical Study of 100 Silent Film Actors and Actresses.* University Press of Kentucky.

[13] Villecco, *Silent Stars Speak.*

[14] Ibid.

[15] "Miss Wagner's Up-To-Date Vaudeville and Movie Gossip." *The Lima News* (OH), June 2, 1921.

[16] Wooldrige, A.L. "Their Phantom Husbands." *Picture Play,* January 1931 [17] "Weighed and Found Wanting – Movie Actress Seeking Divorce." *The Buffalo Courier* (NY), September 6, 1922.

[18] "Gladys Walton Has Her Manager Seized As Thief." The *Brooklyn Daily Eagle,* September 2, 1922.

[19] "Alan Alexander Freed." *Variety,* October 6, 1922.

[20] "Priscilla Bonner's Decree." *Variety,* December 30, 1925.

[21] *Variety,* February 2, 1927.

[22] Slide, Anthony (2005). *Silent Topics: Essays on Undocumented Areas of Silent Film.* Scarecrow Press.

[23] "Screen Debutantes." *Picture-Play,* January 1924.

[24] Villecco, *Silent Stars Speak.*

[25] Slide, *Silent Players.*

[26] Villecco, *Silent Stars Speak.*

[27] "Priscilla Bonner Settles." *Variety,* February 16, 1927.

[28] Slide, *Silent Players.*

[29] Campbell, William. "The Red Kimona." *Motion Picture News,* January 2, 1926.

[30] Fred. "The Red Kimona." *Variety,* February 3, 1926.

[31] "The Shadow Stage." *Photoplay,* March 1926.

[32] *Variety,* July 13, 1927.

[33] Brownlow, Kevin (1968). *The Parade's Gone By . . .* University of California Press.

[34] Reid, Laurence. "The Strong Man." *Motion Picture News,* September 18, 1926.

[35] Ibid.

[36] "The Picture Parade." *Motion Picture,* December 1926

[37] Stenn, David (1988). *Clara Bow: Runnin' Wild.* Cooper Square Press.

[38] Slide, *Silent Players.*

[39] Stenn, *Clara Bow: Runnin' Wild.*

[40] "The Shadow Stage." *Photoplay,* June 1927.

[41] "The Picture Parade." *Motion Picture,* July 1927.

[42] Brownlow, *The Parade's Gone By . . .*

43 Ganly, Raymond. "Paying the Price." *Motion Picture News,* June 10, 1927.

44 "Paying the Price." *Variety,* June 1, 1927.

45 "California, County Marriages, 1850-1952," database with images, FamilySearch (https://FamilySearch.org/ark:/61903/1:1:K8NH-N8F : accessed August 17 2015), Jerome B Chaffee and Marjorie Bonner,

13 Sep 1924; citing Los Angeles, California, United States, county courthouses, California; FHL microfilm 2,074,510.

46 Schallert, Edwin and Elza. "Hollywood High Lights." *Picture Play,* April 1930.

47 "New York, New York City Municipal Deaths, 1795-1949," database, FamilySearch (https://FamilySearch.org/ark:/61903/1:1:2WKH-6JY : accessed August 18 2015), Jerome Burt Chaffee Jr., 05 Oct 1932; citing Death, Manhattan, New York, New York, United States, New York Municipal Archives, New York; FHL microfilm 2,069,936.

48 Bowker, Gordon (1995). *Pursued by Furies: A Life of Malcolm Lowry.* St. Martin's Press.

49 Ancestry.com. UK and Ireland, Find A Grave Index, 1300s-Current [database online]. Provo, UT, USA: Ancestry.com Operations, Inc., 2012. Find A Grave. http://www.findagrave.com/cgi-bin/fg.cgi

50 Grace, Sherrill. "Margerie Bonner's Three Forgotten Novels." *Journal of Modern Literature,* Vol. 6, No. 2 (Apr., 1977), pp. 321-324. Web. Accessed July 7, 2015. < http://www.jstor.org/stable/3831175>

51 Marks, Jason. "The ' Hell in Paradise' of Malcolm Lowry." *New York Times,* October 14, 1973.

52 Grace, "Margerie Bonner's Three Forgotten Novels."

53 "100 Best Novels 1900-1998." *Modern Library.* Web. Accessed July 29, 2015. http://www.modernlibrary.com/top-100/100-best-novels/

54 Bowker, Gordon. "Foul Play at White Cottage." *Times Literary Supplement,* February 20, 2004.

55 Ibid.

56 "Margerie Lowry, 83, Actress and a Writer." *New York Times,* October 4, 1988.

57 "Broadway After Midnight." *The Film Daily,* November 13, 1927.

58 "Outcast Souls." *The Film Daily,* February 5, 1928.

59 "California, County Marriages, 1850-1952," database with images, FamilySearch (https://FamilySearch.org/ark:/61903/1:1:K8NL-P92 : accessed July 28 2015), E Bertrand Woolfan and Priscilla Bonner, 01 Sep 1928; citing Los Angeles, California, United States, county courthouses, California; FHL microfilm 2,074,728.

60 Villecco, *Silent Stars Speak.*

61 Ibid.

62 Sylvester, Ann. "The Hollywood Sorority." *Picture Play,* March 1929.

63 Slide, *Silent Players.*

64 Oliver, Myrna. "Priscilla Bonner, `20s Star of Silent Film." *Los Angeles Times,* February 26, 1996.

## Other Sources:

"Marriage Has Made Her So Slim She Can't Get Work, Movie Star Tells Court In Petitioning For Divorce." The *Washington Times* (DC), August 27, 1922.

Manners, Dorothy. "Club-Night Life in Hollywood." *Motion Picture Classic*, March 1929. Woodcock, George (2007). *Malcolm Lowry: The Man and His Work*. Black Rose Books.

# Chapter 3:
# Grace and Mina Cunard

*Grace (L) and Mina Cunard, Moving Picture World, October 16, 1915. Photo courtesy the Media History Digital Library.*

Most folks' knowledge of the silent film era boils down to three main images: Chaplin's "Little Tramp," custard pie fights, and the woman tied to the railroad tracks. That the latter endures today over a hundred years later is a testament to the immense popularity of the serial. At their apex in the teens, the theaters were a smorgasbord of weekly adventures crammed with nefarious villains, complex plots, and death-defying stunts. As varied as they were, they shared one common denominator: leading women. These were no damsels in distress! They were smart, feisty women kicking butt and taking names, starting with Mary Fuller and Kathlyn Williams and continuing with Helen Holmes, Pearl White, Ruth Roland, Cleo Madison, "Fearless" Florence La Badie . . . and the Queen of the Serials herself, Grace Cunard.

*Mina sporting Pickfordesque curls.* Moving Picture World, *March 25, 1916. Photo courtesy the* Media History Digital Library.

Her Majesty's beginnings were humble. Despite early publicity saying she was born in Paris, she entered the world as Harriet Mildred Jeffries from Columbus, Ohio, April 8, 1893[1]. Mom Lola was a homemaker originally from Missouri; dad Washington was a grocery clerk and native Ohioan. She shared her childhood home with little sister Armina Emma, born December 16, 1894, and Quincy Boling, Lola's son from her short-lived first marriage[2] (born only seven months after her 1881 wedding to Elmer Boling, but you didn't hear it from me)[3][4].

Young Harriet began stage work at thirteen, cycling through stock companies, legitimate theater, and Vaudeville in productions such as *Princess of Patches*. Her first screen credit, widely believed to be *The Duke's Plan* for Biograph in 1910, introduced Grace Cunard—her stage name taken from the steamship lines.[5]

Unlike her sister, Mina never set foot on the stage. She married molder Reuben Kellner in 1911[6], marking her age as twenty-two instead of her tender sixteen. By May 1912, she bore a son, Wilferd[7], mercifully called "Bill," and soon after entered films, likely at Grace's suggestion. Her first credit was *And They Called Him Hero*, for 101 Bison, written by Grace and directed by costar Francis Ford. *Motion Picture News* had mixed feelings, finding it technically pleasing but "gruesome" and "hopelessly unfathomable" during the battle scenes.[8] She earned a flattering writeup from *Moving Picture World*, emphasizing "the family talent" over her lack of experience, and that "her roles [were] growing in importance all the time."[9] Right on its heels came another war story for Bison, *The Doorway of Destruction*, also starring and directed by Francis Ford but also featuring his brother Jack,[*] who co-wrote the scenario with Grace.

Carl Laemmle founded one of the first independent film studios, Independent Motion Pictures (IMP), in 1909. By 1911, he was successful enough to expand to the West, hiring former actor Thomas Ince to run IMP's California studio, as well as direct. Ince departed IMP by 1912, ending up at Bison (a division of the New York Motion Picture Company) and bought Miller Bros. 101 Ranch and Wild West Show, replete with all the sets, props, and "talented, authentic cowboys and Indians"[10] they could want. 101-Bison was thus lauded for their detailed Westerns, so much so that Laemmle moved a unit to Inceville. Francis Ford worked for Ince during this period, juggling the triple duties of actor, writer, and director.

Even though they enjoyed a relatively free creative atmosphere, there was still friction. Head honcho (and main shareholder) Ince often minimized Ford's achievements at the studio or claimed them as his own. About the same time, Laemmle also co-founded the Universal Film Manufacturing

Corp, effectively consolidating IMP, Victor, and Nestor into one cohesive company. (He would acquire Nestor Ranch two years later.) Ford saw his chance and jumped ship for Laemmle's company. Grace joined Universal, too, after freelancing for Biograph and Kalem, and the two began the most rewarding period of their lives. After a short time serving as 101-Bison's leading lady, Mina came along, too.

The first quirky character to spring from Grace's fertile mind was Lady Raffles, jewel thief extraordinaire and star of an eight-film franchise. The mysteries surrounding the "delightfully reckless"[11] heroine crackled with "virility, action, and sparkling plots,"[12] like the organized crime, police raids, and car chases that packed *The Mysterious Hand* (Lady Raffles #5). Both Grace and Francis Ford co-directed, as well as starred. The intrepid duo then took a break from thievery to co-write the spy thriller, *Lucille Love, Girl*

---

*future Academy Award-winning director John Ford.

*Grace and Francis Ford reviewing scripts for* The Broken Coin. Pictures and the Picturegoer, *November 27, 1915. Photo courtesy the* Media History Digital Library.

*of Mystery.* (Some dispute this; publicity lists the author only as "The Master Pen," and possible writers include Cunard, Cunard and Ford, or novelization author

Edwin Bliss.[13]) Originally envisioned as a one-off Western, viewers followed Lucille (Grace) around the globe as she strove to recover vitally important papers stolen from her father by his vengeful former rival Loubeque (Ford). Lasting fifteen parts, many of them ending in nail-biting cliffhangers, *Lucille Love* proved them "unsurpassed in their ability" to keep an audience at the edge of their seats. Ford directed, with his brother John serving as production assistant.

Reporter Kitty Gray finds half of an old coin, covered in Latin, in an antique shop. Translated, it offers up hints of the Kingdom of Gretzhoffen and its hidden treasure. Remembering a past article she wrote about Gretzhoffen teetering on bankruptcy, she wagers her editor a year's salary that she can crack the case and come back with a hell of a story besides. This was *The Broken Coin*, Cunard and Ford's worldwide smash serial, with Grace as Gray, and Ford as both "Count Frederick" and the director. John Ford was assistant director and Grace wrote the scenario, based on a story by Emerson Hough. Torture chambers, royal intrigue, dirigibles vs. submarines in the "greatest battle scene ever staged"[14] . . . this one had everything, and to say it was popular is an understatement. Demand was so prodigious that Universal added six more episodes, twenty-two in total, and issued an estimated 6 million promotional tie-in coins, some of which still turn up in antique markets. Mina even got in on the act, doubling for her sister, [15] as well as playing the small role of "king's sweetheart."

Grace and Francis would simply not have been able to yield the same kind of extraordinary results apart. "It is comparatively easy to write for myself and Francis Ford," Grace admitted, "as we have acted together for so long and understand each other's good and bad points so well."[16] This was unusual for audiences who rarely saw that kind of working intimacy outside of marriage. While no reports of a romance between the two circulated in fan magazines, the chemistry was obvious to everyone, especially Mrs. Ford, who filed for divorce in February 1915, naming Grace as co- respondent. The case was thrown out of court.[17][18] (There is modern speculation that they were lovers, but it remains unverified.)

Mina's resume for Universal was ordinary; still, there was gold hidden among the dross of Westerns, dramas, and farces she churned through. She joined the cast of *Graft* (1915), a serial about a DA's son fighting against the corruption responsible for his father's murder. Hobart Henley starred but injuries sustained in an auto accident[19] led to his being shifted to a supporting role, replaced by Harry Carey. The "well-constructed" and "stirring"[20] political drama boasted stories written by some of the best in the business: playwright and acclaimed George Washington biographer Rupert Hughes; popular Western author Zane Grey; and "mother of the detective novel" Anna Katherine Green, among others. It lasted twenty lucrative episodes.

Best-known today as the father of actress Gloria DeHaven, as well as for *Character Studies* (1927), his hilarious farce of celebrity impressions,[*] Carter DeHaven did some of his earliest movie work in the series *Timothy Dobbs, That's Me* (1916). Each two-reel film featured DeHaven as Dobbs who, thanks to a "remarkable resemblance to Carter DeHaven," sets out for Hollywood and stardom in the pictures. Preposterous situations at the studios— in Episode 8, *Borrowed Plumes*, he dresses as a woman to try and flirt his way to a contract—brought the laughs. Mina was featured in two episodes of the comedy promoted as a wholesome, clean alternative to other shorts. *Motion Picture News* called it "a winner," though Wallace Beery, wearing the director's hat, earned only "adequate."[21]

"The photoplay is supposed to be a visualized sermon of warning . . . told with the completeness of unsavory detail that marks the proceedings at a coroner's inquest."[22] So scrawled a repulsed Ben H. Grimm about *Is Any Girl Safe?* (1916), a cautionary tale on white slavery produced by "The Anti-Vice Motion Picture Company." Mina starred in a story of a factory girl rescued from a forced life of ill repute by the eleventh-hour moral awakening of her captor. Interspersed were scenes of New York's "Potter's Field," where prostitutes' bodies were "shoveled into trenches . . . by convicts," and images of the incarcerated Yushe Botwin, "king of the white slaves."[23] Tying the whole lurid mess together were cutbacks to a minister's sermon on the importance of avoiding such shame.

Sex sold, and police were needed to control the titillated crowds (no one under sixteen admitted) mobbing the box office.

---

[*] Famous for being the only time Buster Keaton and Harold Lloyd appeared on camera together, as well as Keaton's last appearance with Roscoe Arbuckle.

Folks turned away from the initial showing happily waited over two hours for the next one. Community leaders from women's leagues, religious organizations, and related charities like the Home for Wayward Girls were expressly invited to the premiere; sociologists proclaimed it "the most vivid and thorough portrayal of the methods of white slavery"[24] to date.

Maybe a little too thorough. Grimm felt it "[had] no place on the moving picture screen,"[25] and a week after its opening Commissioner of Licenses George H. Bell demanded it banned. By December 1916 it was prohibited from any further screenings in New York under penalty of license revocation.[26][27]

Mina's next film, the melodrama *The Star Witness* (1917), was the polar opposite: a child defends her father in court against erroneous shoplifting charges. It was typical schmaltz, but playing the earnest daughter was nine-year-old Lena Baskette[28], newly signed and years away from her more exotic incarnation of Lina Basquette.

Mina was promoted strangely. On one hand, she tried to carve her own niche by using her birth name, then a completely different stage name altogether; on the other, publicity never wasted an opportunity to remind readers whose sister she was. With articles like "Grace Cunard's Sister is Now Leading Woman in 101 Bison,"[29] what was the point of Mina Jeffries or Margaret Mayburn? Embracing the family connection, she returned to Cunard by April 1916.

*Lucille Love* (1914)and *The Broken Coin* (1915)shot Grace and Ford to Universal's summit, and an admiring public made them the studio's top box-office draw. It was an auspicious time to be making serials, and in response to their profitability, new hierarchical production methods were introduced. Suddenly, jacks-of-all-trades like Ford and Grace were forced to report to "central producers" as well as ancillaries like editors and location scouts.

During *The Adventures of Peg O' the Ring*, their 1916 serial filled with "the charm of the dangers and daring of the circus arena,"[30] Ford and Grace greatly resented the constant "supervision" and interference provided by Laemmle's nephews. They left, were cajoled back, but after the mystery chapter-play, *The Purple Mask*, the

*Amazing Grace.* Motion Picture, *May 1915. Photo courtesy the* Media History
Digital Library.

spell was broken. Grace continued to act but no longer produced or directed; this was quite the blow for a woman whose combined efforts amounted to a "four-figure salary every week."[31] Ford directed some, but by 1918 he left Universal altogether.

1917 was a year of orange blossoms and rice for both young women. In January, only two months after their first meeting, Grace eloped with Joseph Moore of the famed Moore acting dynasty (brothers Tom, Matt, and Owen were all actors, as was sister Mary). *Photoplay* hyperbolized it was the "greatest matrimonial sensation that has come out of filmland for several eons,"[32] possibly since Owen's 1911 marriage to Mary Pickford. Mina also became a blushing bride for the second time later that year. (She and Kellner divorced sometime in 1916.) Husband #2 was Universal property chief and camera operator Stockton Quincy,[33] who'd previously acted for Kalem and Gaumont. The two tied the knot just before Quincy, a member of the U.S. Army Coast Artillery Corps, shipped out for camp.[34]

Stress, exhaustion, and repeated injuries compelled Grace to withdraw from the adventure serial *Elmo the Fearless* (1920), starring Elmo Lincoln (cinema's first Tarzan). Louise Lorraine, in her film debut, replaced her. Though she made a full recovery and worked steadily through the 1920s, the roles were nowhere at her previous level. One blissful result of her frequent appearance in Westerns was her September 1925 marriage to actor Jack Shannon,[35] former rodeo rider and stunt double for Tom Mix, William S. Hart, and Hoot Gibson. (The great Moore-Cunard matrimonial sensation ended earlier that year.)

After *A Beach Nut* (1919), a comedy short written, directed by, and starring Wallace Beery, Mina retired from films. Already divorced from Quincy, she married prolific bit actor Harold Cohen, a.k.a. Harry Seymour, in February of 1920[36] and devoted herself to home life. There's little about Wilferd/"Bill" during these years, other than living with his maternal grandmother in Los Angeles[37], but both he and Lola were living with Harry and Mina by the early 1930s.[38] (Bill married dancer Pearl Hobson in 1934.[39]) Mina occasionally appeared with Harry during his tenure as WSMB radio announcer, where they sang on-air as "Mr. and Mrs. Gloom-

*Bathing beauty Mina. Motion Picture, July 1917. Photo courtesy the Media History Digital Library.*

chaser."[40] In 1942, Harry and Mina legally changed their names to Seymour,[41] but it was under Cunard that Mina re-entered films, with a bit part as a welder in the WWII picture *Good Luck Mr. Yates*(1943), which originally had The Three Stooges performing the Vaudeville classic, "Niagara Falls," but the sequence was cut before release. Columbia salvaged the footage and released it as the short *Gents Without Cents* in 1944.[42] Mina's unaccredited extra work lasted until *The Gift of Love* (1958), when she retired from films permanently. She moved to the Motion Picture Country House after Harry's death in 1967, and died there at age 83 on August 9, 1978.[43]

Grace spent the 1930s and 1940s helping to raise James, Jack's son from his previous marriage, and making unaccredited appearances in films such as *Ladies They Talk About* (1933), *Bride of Frankenstein* (1935), *Show Boat* (1936), and *A Little Bit of Heaven* (1940). She ended her pioneering career with the Ginger Rogers/David Niven historical drama *Magnificent Doll* (1946). Even though her cinematic heyday was already considered forgotten, she still received "a thousand inquiries from [those] who remember Grace Cunard and her hair-raising adventures."[44] By the end of her life, she was also a resident of the Motion Picture Country House, and it was there cancer claimed her on January 19, 1967.[45] She was 73.

[1] Ancestry.com. California, Death Index, 1940-1997 [database on-line]. Provo, UT, USA: Ancestry.com Operations Inc, 2000. Original data: information for Grace M Cunard, State of California. California Death Index, 1940-1997. Sacramento, CA, USA: State of California Department of Health Services, Center for Health Statistics. Accessed April 29, 2015.

[2] "United States Census, 1900," index and images, FamilySearch (https://familysearch.org/ark:/61903/1:1:MMZB-QM1 : accessed April 28, 2015), Harriet M Jeffries in household of Washington Jeffries, Montgomery Township, Precinct A Columbus City Ward 17, Franklin, Ohio, United States; citing sheet 11A, family 242, NARA microfilm publication T623 (Washington, D.C.: National Archives and Records Administration, n.d.); FHL microfilm 1,241,269.

[3] "Ohio, Marriages, 1800-1958," index, FamilySearch (https://familysearch.org/ark:/61903/1:1:XDNV-FX8 : accessed May 1, 2015), E. E. Boling and L. M. Longshore, 10 Jan 1881; citing Holmes,Ohio, reference ; FHL microfilm 0477146 V. 6-7.

[4] "Ohio, Deaths, 1908-1953," index and images, FamilySearch (https://familysearch.org/ark:/61903/1:1:X8FW-1XV : accessed May 1, 2015), Lola M. Longshore in entry for Quiney Allen Boling, 23 Nov 1914; citing Columbus, Franklin, Ohio, reference fn 60270; FHL microfilm 1,983,284.

[5] Birchard, Robert S. (2009). Early Universal City (Images of America). Arcadia Publishing.

[6] "Kentucky Marriages, 1785-1979," index, FamilySearch (https://familysearch.org/ark:/61903/1:1:F4MJ-NMH : accessed April 25, 2015), Reuben Kellner and Armina Jeffries, 27 Mar 1911; citing Kenton County, Kentucky, reference v 42 p 85; FHL microfilm 551,112.

[7] National Archives and Records Administration. U.S. World War II Army Enlistment Records, 1938-1946[database on- line]. Provo, UT, USA: Ancestry.com Operations Inc, 2005. Original data: Electronic Army Serial Number Merged File, 1938-1946 [Archival Database]; ARC: 1263923. World War II Army Enlistment Records; Records of the National Archives and Records Administration, Record Group 64; National Archives at College Park. College Park, Maryland, U.S.A. Accessed April 20, 2015.

[8] "And They Called Him Hero." Motion Picture News, April 10, 1915.

[9] "Mina Jeffries." The Moving Picture World, March 25, 1916.

[10] Dirks, Tim. "The History of Film – The Pre-1920s." AMC Filmsite. Web. Accessed April 19, 2015. http://www.filmsite.org/pre20sintro3.html

[11] Bean, Jennifer M.. "Grace Cunard." In Jane Gaines, Radha Vatsal, and Monica Dall'Asta, eds. *Women Film Pioneers Project*. Center for Digital Research and Scholarship. New York, NY: Columbia University Libraries, 2013. Web. Accessed April 14, 2015. https://wfpp.cdrs.columbia.edu/pioneer/ccp-grace-cunard/

[12] "The Mysterious Hand." *The Moving Picture World*, October 17, 1914.

13 "Lucille Love, The Girl of Mystery; or: Lost in the Yukon." Classic Film Aficionados Wordpress, 17 September 2014. Web. Accessed April 20, 2015. http://classicfilmafi-cionados.com/2014/09/17/lucille-love-the-girl-of-mystery-or-lost-in-the-yukon/

[14] Heisley, *The 14th Episode of the Broken Coin: $10,000 Production Put on by Universal Film Co. at Venice, Sunday, July 25th, Promptly at Noon : Greatest Battle Scene Ever Staged : Absolute Destruction of a Monster Fort by a Dirigible, Sinking of Large War Cruise, Battle between 2 Submarines, Over 1200 Men in Action ... Actual Submarines, a Real Cruiser, a Monster Dirigible and a Fort 60 Feet Square and 25 Feet High : the Greatest Event Ever Staged Anywhere : on the Sands at the Foot of Westminster Street in Venice : Take Pacific Electric Cars, 4th and Hill Street Station*. Los Angeles?: publisher not identified, 1915. Print. (A poster to urge crowds to come and watch the filming of a battle scene. Illustration signed: Heisley.) *Worldcat*. Web. Accessed April 15, 2015. http://www.worldcat.org/oclc/54633937

[15] Wollstein, Hans J. "Mina Cunard." *All Movie Guide*. Web. Accessed April 9, 2015. http://www.allmovie.com/artist/mina-cunard-p16178

[16] Willis, Richard. "Chats With the Players: Grace Cunard, of the Universal Company." *Motion Picture*, July 1915.

[17] "Wife Names Grace Cunard." *Variety*, February 12, 1915.

[18] "Ford Divorce Denied." *Variety*, February 20, 1915.

[19] *The Moving Picture World*, December 18, 1915.

[20] "Universal Film Mfg. Company Specials." *The Moving Picture World*, December 11, 1915.

[21] Milne, Peter. "Timothy Dobbs – That's Me." *Motion Picture News*, August 19, 1916.

[22] Grimm, Ben H. "Is Any Girl Safe?" *The Moving Picture World*, September 23, 1916.

[23] "'Is Any Girl Safe?' Released." *Motography*, September 30, 1916.

[24] Ibid.

[25] Grimm, "Is Any Girl Safe?"

[26] "Scored National Censor Board." The *New York Clipper*, October 7, 1916.

[27] "Two More Banned." *Variety*, December 15, 1916.

[28] "The Star Witness." *Motion Picture News*, April 14, 1917.

[29] "Grace Cunard's Sister is Now Leading Woman in 101 Bison." *Motion Picture News*, March 18, 1916.

[30] Advertisement in *The Moving Picture World*, July 1, 1916, pg. 7.

[31] Mahar, Karen Ward (2008). *Women Filmmakers in Early Hollywood (Studies in Industry and Society)*. Johns Hopkins University Press.

[32] York, Cal. "Plays and Players." *Photoplay*, April 1917.

[33] "California, County Marriages, 1850-1952," index and images, FamilySearch (https://familysearch.org/ark:/61903/1:1:XLCS-J58 : accessed April 18,  2015),

Stockton Quincy and Armina E Jeffries, 13 Sep 1917; citing Los Angeles, California, United States, county courthouses, California; FHL microfilm 1,033,269.

34 York, Cal. "Plays and Players." *Photoplay,* December 1917.

35"California, County Marriages, 1850-1952," index and images, FamilySearch (https://familysearch.org/ark:/61903/1:1:K8ND-SMK : accessed April 18, 2015), Frederick L Tyler and Harriet M Jeffries, 01 Sep 1925; citing Los Angeles, California, United States, county courthouses, California; FHL microfilm 2,074,522.

36 "California, County Marriages, 1850-1952," index and images, FamilySearch (https://familysearch.org/ark:/61903/1:1:K8Z5-GXL : accessed May 1, 2015), Harold Coken and Armina Kellner, 10 Feb 1920; citing Los Angeles, California, United States, county courthouses, California; FHL microfilm 2,074,213.

37 Year: 1920; Census Place: Los Angeles Assembly District 74, Los Angeles, California; Roll: T625_115; Page:1B; Enumeration District: 425; Image: 78. Ancestry.com. 1920 United States Federal Census [database on-line]. Provo, UT, USA: Ancestry.com Operations Inc, 2010. Images reproduced by FamilySearch.

38 Year: 1930; Census Place: Bronx, Bronx, New York; Roll: 1467; Page: 1B; Enumeration District: 0147; Image:669.0; FHL microfilm: 2341202. Ancestry.com. 1930 United States Federal Census [database on-line]. Provo, UT, USA: Ancestry.com Operations Inc, 2002.

39 "California, County Marriages, 1850-1952," index and images, FamilySearch (https://familysearch.org/ark:/61903/1:1:K8J6-33Q : accessed May 1, 2015), Wilfred Otto Kellner and Pearl Louise Hobson, 17 Jan 1934; citing Los Angeles, California, United States, county courthouses, California; FHL microfilm 2,075,114.

40 Block, Moise M. "Broadcast Artists Wind Up WSMB Sunday Night Frolic With Coffee." *Radio Digest,* February 1931.

41 Cohen, Harry and Armina. Order Changing Name, No. 475882, June 9, 1942, Los Angeles, CA. Legal document scanned and added to Armina Emma Jeffries family tree 4 Jun 2012, by "beachman0 ". Accessed via Ancestry.com April 13, 2015. http://trees.ancestry.com/tree/1737607/person/1808990168

42 "Good Luck Mr. Yates." *The Three Stooges Online Filmography.* n.d. Web. Accessed April 17, 2015. http://www.threestooges.net/filmography/episode/462

44 Cunard, Grace. "Crowded Out of Stardom." *New Movie Magazine,* February 1932.

45 "Obituary: Grace Cunard, 73, Silent Film Star." *New York Times,* January 24, 1967.

## Other Sources:

Hinkson, Jake. "Serial Queens of the Silent Era: The First Female Action Heroes." *Tor.com.* December 13, 2013. Web. Accessed May 3, 2015. http://www.tor.com/2013/12/13/the-first-female-action-heroes/

*Motion Picture News,* January 29, 1916.

"Pacific Coast Notes." *Motography,* April 8, 1916.

"Tabloid Reviews for the Busy Exhibitor." *Motion Picture News,* July 29, 1916.

*The Broken Coin.* 2007. Web. Accessed April 22, 2015. http://www.thebrokencoin.com

# Chapter 4:
# Alice and Marceline Day

*Marceline (L) and Alice Day,* Photoplay, *January 1926. Photo courtesy the* Media History Digital Library.

It was 1910, and Frank and Irene Newlin were newly divorced.[1] There wasn't much left in Pueblo, Colorado, for the twenty-four-year-old mother of two, so she packed up daughters Alice and

Marceline and headed for the security of her mother and stepfather in Cripple Creek[2]. Going home wasn't easy; she'd run away at sixteen precisely to escape the "humiliations heaped upon her by a tyrannical mother."[3] It took four years for Irene to find stability again, with Salt Lake City accountant Edgar J. Blackwell. She and the girls moved to Utah[4] to start a new life, one that lasted into the early 1920s.

How or why the Blackwell ladies wound up in California is ambiguous, but by 1924 they'd left Utah (and Mr. Blackwell) and settled there under the new surname Day. "We didn't want to be movie stars," Marceline confessed in an interview. "Alice and I wanted to finish high school, but mother insisted on our trying the pictures first."[5] Irene was a graduate of the Peg Talmadge School of Parenting, determined, perhaps because of her own struggles, to raise independently wealthy daughters who needed men only for companionship. As long as they brought in a pretty penny, she wasn't against them flaunting it a bit either: "[c]ertainly, buy fur coats . . . [y]ou're making your own money. Make the most of it."[6] They repaid her guidance by "saving towards an annuity for their mother, 'because Mother wouldn't want to be dependent on our husbands.'"[7]

Both young ladies started as Sennett Bathing Beauties in 1923. Alice and Marceline were unaccredited window-dressing in Harry Langdon's *Picking Peaches* (1924), and Marceline supported him in two other shorts that year. Alice also sparkled as Langdon's leading lady in five shorts, often opposite vampy Madeline Hurlock. She then teamed with Ben Turpin for *Romeo and Juliet*, while Marceline starred in the Sid Smith comedy *Black Oxfords*.

By the end of 1924, Alice's "talent for facial double takes and expressions"[8] made her the perfect companion to Ralph Graves in a new Sennett romantic comedy series focused on a young couple's adventures. Previously, Graves matched up beautifully with Mabel Normand in *The Extra Girl* (1923), so Alice, "the closest thing Sennett had come across in terms of a Mabel Normand-styled comedienne,"[9] was ideal. She was in seven of the twelve two-reelers, starting with *East of the Water Plug* (1924) with Vernon Dent and

*Alice and Ralph Graves in* East of the Water Plug. Motion Picture, *September 1924. Photo courtesy the* Media History Digital Library.

Billy Bevan, and ending with *Bashful Jim* (1925). It was dessert entertainment, frothy and light, with lots of recycled gags.

At the same time, Alice built her reputation as a funny lady alongside Ben Turpin (*The Reel Virginian*, 1924), Langdon again (*The Sea Squawk*, 1925), and Raymond McKee (*Honeymoon Hardships*, 1925). The last one gave audiences a preview of Sennett's next big thing for Pathé: Alice Day Comedies. The "champion picker of comedians"[10] saw her potential and headlined her in three 1925 comedies, all costarring Raymond McKee. A shiny new contract guaranteed $350 per week. The first one, *Tee for Two*, veneered an evergreen plot—poor girl wins rich boy's heart despite obstacle—with golf, but it was no hole-in-one. Alice appeared "self-conscious"[11] and "sweet but not funny,"[12] and an overemphasis on romance bogged the pace down to "a slow-motion walk."[13]

It was quickly followed by *Cold Turkey*, a newlywed slapstick farce, and *Love and Kisses*, "nothing more than a condensation of the first Normand feature, *Mickey*."[14]

As the series progressed, Alice changed love interests, from McKee to Danny O'Shea, Joe Young, and Eddie Quillan. Up to this point, almost all were directed by Eddie Cline, but starting in June 1926 comedian Larry Semon took the wheel for two shorts, *The Plumber's Daughter* (1927) and Alice's penultimate short, *Pass the Dumplings* (1927). Her final short was *A Dozen Socks* (1927), a prizefighting comedy with regulars Quillan, O'Shea, and Barney Hellum, after which both Sennett and Alice were ready to move on to new adventures.

Marceline, meanwhile, was busy at Universal, supporting Arthur Lake in his comedy series and appearing in Westerns with Jack Hoxie and Art Acord. She freelanced for several studios through 1926: 20th Century Fox, Frank Lloyd Productions, and MGM, where she earned top billing for the first time in *The Boy Friend*, a "clever satire"[15] of the rules of romance costarring John Harron.

She also headlined two films for Tiffany Productions, *That Model from Paris* and *College Days*. Though her work wasn't as visible as Alice's, she attracted enough attention to result in a contract with MGM and a nomination as a WAMPAS Baby Star of 1926. This was their exceptional year: Mary Astor, Dolores Costello, Joan Crawford, Dolores del Rio, Janet Gaynor, and Fay Wray were among the others chosen.

Her first role in 1927 was a plum one for United Artists. *The Beloved Rogue* starred John Barrymore as François Villon, legendary fifteenth century French poet, in a dashing story of love and adventure. Marceline was Charlotte, ward of King Louis XVI (Conrad Veidt in his Hollywood debut) and object of Villon's desire. *The Beloved Rogue* was lavishly shot, with many of the exteriors reused from *The Hunchback of Notre Dame* (1923). Barrymore arrogantly insisted eighteen-year-old Marceline didn't comprehend the socio-political undertones to Villon's story and turned in an "absolutely wooden"[16] performance. Audiences didn't care much for erudite swashbuckling; reviews called it "sure-fire hokum,"[17] but attendance was primarily by ardent Barrymore fans. Marceline was well aware for whom the movie was: "[T]he prestige will help me—but there won't be much me in the picture, will there?"[18]

The history of the first "gospel ship" promised little excitement, but *Captain Salvation* (1927) surprisingly delivered. The film belonged to Lars Hanson as a divinity student who rescues a prostitute (an electric Pauline Starke) from a cruel captain (Ernest Torrence), then turns the ship into the first floating ministry. Marceline does little but look pretty as Hanson's love interest, but the moving, "well- knit drama"[19] was great for her resume.

Alice's costar at First National was more simian than seminarian: *The Gorilla* (1927) spoofed "old dark house" thrillers like that year's *The Cat and the Canary.* Alice's father is murdered and the prime suspect is, yes, a gorilla. Is he real? Someone in a rubber suit? Is there one of each wreaking havoc? More mirthful than macabre thanks to Charlie Murray and Fred Kelsey, *The Gorilla* cleaned up as successfully at the box office as it had on stage and sent viewers into "tumult[s] of chills and laughter."[20] Today, the film is mostly remembered for the ape costume, the first designed by future Hollywood "Ape Man" Charles Gemora, and for the iconic shot of Alice, clad in a pure white negligee (no symbolism there), being carried off by the frightening beast.

Hollywood's view of youth was split into fun-loving flappers like Clara Bow and Joan Crawford, and virtuous ingénues who made Mary Pickford look like a party animal. Alice and Marceline were squarely in the second camp, and their publicity rammed it hard down readers' throats. "They are just like two convent misses," remarked one columnist, "jolly and charming in their nice, quiet little way."[21]

*John Barrymore and Marceline in* The Beloved Rogue. Picture Play, *April 1927. Photo courtesy the* Media History Digital Library.

The girls dated—Alice linked to Carl Laemmle Jr., Marceline to Richard Dix—but it was all presented as chaste and wholesome. Neither daughter smoked, drank, or got embroiled in scandal. Mom Irene was never far, and often depicted as younger and more vivacious "than her two rather staid daughters."[22] The denizens of

*From L to R: Alice, Marceline, and mom Irene.* Photoplay, *June 1929. Photo courtesy the* Media History Digital Library.

La La Land thought she was the bees' knees, definitely not "the kind of movie mother that only a daughter could love."[23] All of this sweetness and light makes them sound as exciting as a root canal, but don't count them out yet.

Alice, whose big eyes and "snuggly little figure"[24] painted "a girl for petting and protection,"[25] was a tough contract negotiator and expert equestrian. Marceline, as tall and willowy as her sister was cuddly, had a confident "boyish swagger"[26] and progressive mindset about romance. "Why can't a husband and wife be friends? . . . [L]ive like two pals. Consider one another."[27] They were marvelous entertainers and their get-togethers were always hot with the smart set: "when the Days give a party, you stay partied!"[28] Score one for the straight-laced sisters, "two of the most charming, most loveable kids in town."[29]

Marceline's next job was an unassuming thriller starring Lon Chaney. Modern silent film fans the world over know of *London After Midnight* as the Holy Grail of lost films, but in 1927 it was just another offering from Tod Browning. In the story, five years after his suicide by gunshot, Roger Balfour's home is occupied by a rogues' gallery: his grown daughter Lucille (Day), his neighbor Hamlin (Henry B. Walthall), Hamlin's nephew Arthur (Conrad Nagel), and the hired help (Polly Moran and Percy Williams.) Convinced Balfour was murdered, a disguised Inspector Burke

*Alice and William Haines*, Picture Play, *April 1928. Photo
courtesy the* Media History Digital Library.

(Chaney) and companion (Edna Tichenor) return to the home to
recreate the events before the crime and hopefully expose the
perpetrator. Marceline was second billed but cheated again, "rel-
egated to the background with the love interest."[30]

*Variety* felt Chaney played Burke too "mechanical and wood-
en,"[31] but as the cadaverous Man in the Beaver Hat was "right at
home in one of his unusual characterizations."[32]  Reviews were
split between "thrills and weird doings . . . fine entertainment"[33]
and "not of the quality that results in broken house records."[34]

Alice didn't get much opportunity to expand her repertoire in
1928, but she paid the bills and kept current enough to make the

*Marceline and Ralph Forbes in* Restless Youth. *Exhibitors Herald and Moving Picture World, December 15, 1928. Photo courtesy the Media History Digital Library.*

WAMPAS list that year. She was the girl of William Haines' dreams in *The Smart Set*; the object of Mitchell Lewis' unrequited love in the Frank Capra crime drama *The Way of the Strong*; and Richard Barthlemess' taxing wife in the early talkie *Drag* (1929).

That same year, she appeared in MGM's *Show of Shows* (in the "Meet My Sister" number) and *Is Everybody Happy?* with bandleader Ted Lewis for Warner Bros. Then, she starred in *Times Square*, a Poverty Row musical about Tin Pan Alley. She oscillated between minor parts for First National, Columbia, and Warner Bros. and top billing in B-movies such as *Ladies in Love* (1930) and *The Lady from Nowhere* (1931) for Chesterfield. She received sixth billing at Peerless in *Love Bound* (1932), a.k.a. *Murder on the High Seas*, with former heavyweights Clara Kimball Young and Roy D'Arcy, and after that her career flatlined. The silver lining to the celluloid cloud: it made no difference to Alice. She and Hollywood broker Jack Cohn married on July 6, 1930, and son Richard was born March 10, 1931. After two 1932 Westerns, *Two-Fisted Law* (Columbia) with Tim McCoy and an achingly young John Wayne, and *Gold* (Larry Darmour Productions) with Jack Hoxie, she happily retired to be a full-time wife and mother.

Marceline's stardom traveled much the same path and would've ended in obscurity if not for Buster Keaton. He had just signed a contract with MGM and relinquished creative control for the first time, a move that ended in both professional and personal disaster. At the time of *The Cameraman* (1928), often referred to as his last great silent, the ink was still wet and optimism reigned for him and the studio. Keaton was Buster, a tintype photographer bent on becoming an MGM newsreel cameraman to impress Sally (Day), the secretary at the newsreel office. He achieves his dream (and Sally) thanks to a Tong War, a capuchin monkey, and "[t]he same old stencil about a boob that does everything wrong and cashes in finally through sheer luck."[35]

Reviews liked the "fairly boisterous ... first-rate comedy,"[36] and found Marceline "appealing," but balked a bit at Buster's "cow-like adoration" and "abysmal stupidity"[37] in spots.[*]

Fresh off that success, Marceline reunited that year with Browning and Chaney for *The Big City*, and with Dane and Arthur for *Detectives* (she filmed the comedy *Rookies* with them the year before). Columbia gave her the lead in *Restless Youth*, but the courtroom drama about a college coed with a sordid past did nothing to maintain career momentum. Talkies plus an egregious contract dispute with MGM steadily weakened her cinematic métier. There were bright spots: Clara Bow's first talkie, *The Wild*

*Party* (Paramount, 1929), the aforementioned *Show of Shows*, and the early Douglas

Fairbanks Jr. feature, *The Jazz Age* (FBO, 1929), but the 1930s generally offered the same options as it had her sister.

She did Benny Rubin comedies at Tiffany (one, *Hot Curves*, co-starred Alice); sang a few notes as the desired "white woman" in the adventure *Paradise Island* (1930), and cheapie dramas and Westerns for Chesterfield and Monogram opposite Rex Bell, Conway Tearle, and Ken Maynard.

She married furrier Arthur Klein in 1931, but kept working in whatever was available—and what was available was atrocious. The exploitation drama *Damaged Lives* (Weldon Pictures[†], 1933) made the newly platinum-blonde Marceline a syphilitic prostitute who, after finding out she has unknowingly infected a friend, commits suicide. The uneven adventure *The Flaming Signal* (Imperial, 1933), a vehicle for Flash the Wonder Dog, gave her a topless swimming scene. Both roles were the death knell of her former pristine image, and after one last Western, *The Fighting Parson* (Allied, 1933) with Hoot Gibson, she left the screen for good.

Alice sued Jack for divorce in 1936, citing cruelty; it was finalized by 1939[38], and Alice got full custody of Richard and second son, Gary, born in 1933. Alice resumed her maiden name and both boys adopted the surname Day. At some point during the late 1940s she was married to banker Charles J. Hawkins,[39] but no further information is available. Scott Day, Richard's son, remembers his grandmother living a "very quiet life,"[40] one that had been single for a long time. In later years, she was a nursing volunteer at a local California hospital, and tenderly cared for Richard during a lengthy illness. (Both sons are now deceased.) Alice Day suffered a stroke which led to her death on May 24, 1995[41]. She was 88.

Marceline's first marriage also ended in divorce, but she found happiness with John Arthur, president of Ripley's Believe it or Not, in 1959. After Ripley's death in 1949, Arthur bought the vast majority of his artifacts and opened the first permanent Ripley's museum in Florida in 1950.[42]   He and business partner Doug

---

[†] a false front for Columbia, who didn't want their name associated with the subject matter.

Storer spent the 1950s building the Ripley empire through books, magazines, comics, and additional museums (called "Odditoriums") in Las Vegas, Atlantic City, and New York City. After Storer retired Arthur partnered with T. Alec Rigby to open museums in Canada, San Francisco, and Chicago. By 1969, Rigby was sole owner. Mr. Day fondly remembered Arthur taking him and his siblings to marvel at delights like a replica of Lincoln's log cabin constructed out of pennies.

"Aunt Marcy" and "Uncle John" adored traveling the globe; Marceline even wrote a cookbook for family and friends detailing her gastronomic adventures abroad. Out of all the places they visited, France was her favorite. As to her former career, she was reluctant to discuss it, though Mr. Day recalls mention of Lon Chaney and John Barrymore. It wasn't out of bitterness or heartache, he assured me; quite simply, that part of her life was over, and she preferred to focus on the present.[43]

Marceline and John lived in New York for a while, always returning to California for Christmas.

Eventually they moved to a condo in Palm Springs, where Marceline Day Arthur died of natural causes on February 16, 2000.[44] She was cremated and her ashes spread in Palm Springs by family. She was 91.

[1] Ancestry.com. Colorado, Divorce Index, 1851-1985 [database on-line]. Provo, UT, USA: Ancestry.com Operations, Inc., 2015.

[2] Year: 1910; Census Place: Cripple Creek Ward 3, Teller, Colorado; Roll: T624_125; Page: 1B; Enumeration District: 0196; FHL microfilm: 1374138. Ancestry.com. 1910 United States Federal Census [database on-line]. Provo, UT, USA: Ancestry.com Operations Inc, 2006.

[3] Albert, Katherine. "Home Rules for Hollywood Flappers." *Photoplay*, June 1929.

[4] Year: 1920; Census Place: Cornish, Cache, Utah; Roll: T625_1861; Page: 15A; Enumeration District: 21; Image: 682. Ancestry.com. 1920 United States Federal Census [database on-line]. Provo, UT, USA: Ancestry.com Operations Inc, 2010. Images reproduced by FamilySearch.

[5] Calhoun, Dorothy. "Do Women Rule the Movies?" *Motion Picture Classic*, August 1928.

[6] Albert, "Home Rules for Hollywood Flappers."

[7] Ibid.

[8] Walker, Brent E. (2010). *Mack Sennett's Fun Factory: A History and Filmography of His Keystone and Mack Sennett Comedies with Biographies of Players and Personnel,  Vols. 1 & 2*. McFarland.

[9] Ibid.

[10] Advertisement for Alice Day Comedies in *Exhibitors Trade Review*, August 22, 1925, pg. 41.

[11] Kennedy, Thomas C. "Tee for Two." *Motion Picture News*, August 1, 1925.

[12] "Short Subjects: 'Tee for Two.'" *Film Daily*, July 26, 1925.

[13] Kennedy, "Tee for Two."

[14] Walker, *Mack Sennett's Fun Factory.*

[15] "'The Boy Friend' at Gates." The *Brooklyn Daily Eagle*, August 22, 1926.

[16] Fryer, Paul, and Anna Shoulgat (2004). *In Hollywood with Nemirovich-Danchen-ko1926-1927: The Memoirs of Sergei Bertensson (Studies and Documentation in the History of Popular Entertainment)*. Scarecrow Press.

[17] "The Beloved Rogue." *Film Daily*, March 20, 1927.

[18] Gebhart, Myrtle. "Marceline Keeps Cool." *Picture-Play*, April 1927.

[19] "The Shadow Stage." *Photoplay*, July 1927.

[20] "The Gorilla." *Film Daily*, November 13, 1927.

[21] "Grace Kingsley's Gossip from Hollywood." *Screenland*, June 1928.

[22] Ibid.

[23] "In New York." *Screenland*, July 1928.

[24] Gebhart, "Marceline Keeps Cool."

[25] Johnston, Carol. "The Girl Who Wouldn't Undress." *Motion Picture Classic*, February 1929.

[26] Gebhart, "Marceline Keeps Cool."

[27] Tildesley, Ruth M. "Wanted: A Husband." *Motion Picture*, January 1929.

[28] "Grace Kingsley's Gossip from Hollywood."

[29] Albert, "Home Rules for Hollywood Flappers."

[30] Mort. "London After Midnight." *Variety*, December 14, 1927.

[31] Ibid.

[32] "London After Midnight." *Film Daily*, December 18, 1927.

[33] Ibid.

[34] Mort, "London After Midnight."

[35] Land. "The Cameraman." *Variety*, September 19, 1928.

[36] Reid, Laurence. "The Celluloid Critic." *Motion Picture Classic*, November 1928.

[37] Land, "The Cameraman."

[38] *Cohn v. Cohn*, 47 Cal. App. 2d 683, 118 P.2d 903 (Ct. App. 1941). *Justia: U.S. Law.* Web. Accessed September 18, 2015. http://law.justia.com/cases/california/court-of-appeal/2d/47/683.html

[39] "Former Village Couple Here for Yule Holidays." *Desert Sun* (CA), December 30, 1949.

[40] Day, Scott (September 24, 2015). Phone interview with author.

[41] Ancestry.com. U.S., Social Security Applications and Claims Index, 1936-2007 [database on-line]. Provo, UT, USA: Ancestry.com Operations, Inc., 2015.

[42] Colley, Jessica. "Secrets of Ripley's Believe It or Not." New York.com, September 15, 2014. Web. Accessed Sept 2, 2015. http://www.newyork.com/articles/attractions/secrets-of-ripleys-believe-it-or-not-09896

[43] Day, phone interview.

[44] Number: 105-24-6242; Issue State: New York; Issue Date: Before 1951. Ancestry.com. U.S., Social Security Death Index,1935-2014 [database on-line]. Provo, UT, USA: Ancestry.com Operations Inc, 2011.

## Other Sources:

"Alice Day Married to Broker." New York Times, July 8, 1930.

Ancestry.com. Utah, Select Marriages, 1887-1966 [database on-line]. Provo, UT, USA: Ancestry.com Operations, Inc, 2014. "Believe It or Not." Sponsor, August 24, 1964.

"Colorado Statewide Marriage Index, 1853-2006," database with images, FamilySearch (https://familysearch.org/ark:/61903/1:1:KNQN-6CT : accessed September 3 2015), Frank Newlin and Irene M Freeman, 24

May 1905, Pueblo, Pueblo, Colorado, United States; citing no. 8142, State Archives, Denver; FHL microfilm 1,690,114. "Hawkins Hosts to Mrs. Arthur." Desert Sun (CA), September 24, 1948.

Soister, John, Henry Nicolella, Steve Joyce, William F. Chase, Harry Long (2012). American Silent Horror, Science Fiction and Fantasy Feature Films, 1913-1929. McFarland.

"Son to Alice Day, Screen Actress." New York Times, March 12, 1931.

# Chapter 5:
# Madeline and Marion Fairbanks

*Madeline (L) and Marion Fairbanks, Reel Life, December 20, 1913. Photo courtesy the Media History Digital Library.*

In 1890, a Manhattan stenographer named John Fairbanks and his sweetheart, Jane Mills, tied the knot. A year into their marriage, Jane, called "Jennie," gave birth to their first child, a daughter. They named her Madeleine. Death took Madeleine in April 1892[1] at only five months.

About a year later, a son named Bloomfield was born. Seven years later, the Fairbanks clan welcomed two beautiful baby girl, born only five minutes apart. The happy parents, in bittersweet memory, named the older twin Madeleine; the younger was Marion.[2]

Madeleine and Marion began working on the stage when they were quite young in the evergreen productions you'd expect: *Mrs. Wiggs of the Cabbage Patch*, *Snow White*, and *The Prince Chap*, among others. They joined Vaudeville superstar Nora Bayes in *The Jolly Bachelors* in 1909, and received some of their first press (albeit as Marion and "Marjorie") in 1910 for *The Blue Bird*. Ned Wayburn worked with them in *Bachelors* and would be integral to their career later.

Very little exists on how Dad felt about the twins getting into showbiz, but it didn't matter: Mom's parents wouldn't let her become an actress, and the moment her daughters showed interest she was going to make them famous, come hell or high water.

New York was a movie-making mecca in 1909, with Vitagraph and Biograph doing booming business there. (Edison was also thriving in nearby northern New Jersey.) Edwin Thanhouser, wealthy theater manager, thought it time to toss his hat in the ring. Already familiar with New Rochelle, the Westchester region "forty five minutes from Broadway" and popular with those in entertainment, he bought a vacant skating rink and set about creating a movie studio. Their first film was released March 15, 1910, and before long, Thanhouser carved itself a profitable and critically acclaimed niche among its celluloid competitors.

Madeleine (now Madeline for film purposes) and Marion started their cinematic careers with Biograph in 1910, but as was policy, they were not identified (or publicized) by name. They made their Thanhouser debut in *The Twins* (1912). The girls play orphans, only one of whom is adopted by their crotchety old uncle. Heartbroken, the left-behind sister escapes to the uncle's house, and they scheme to both live there under the ruse of being one child. Spoiler alert: he discovers their deception but, his chilly heart melted by their tears, promises both girls can stay. The sweet, simple story was a hit. The *Morning Telegraph* found it "delightful in every sense," including its stars: "The Thanhouser Twins may be sure of a welcome wherever they appear."[3]

Thanhouser's roster shone with big name talent. Director James Cruze began there as an actor. Stage luminary Maude Fealy acted and wrote scenarios. Their biggest star, Florence La Badie, was dubbed "Fearless Flo" for her stunt work; her early death at the height of her game was one of film's first tragedies. Muriel Ostriche gained notoriety as the "Moxie" girl, appearing in ads for the soft drink. Among the younger set, the Thanhouser Twins headed the trifecta, along with Marie Eline, the Thanhouser Kid, and Helen Badgley, the Thanhouser Kidlet. They were well-liked by all at the studio, who assigned different colored ribbons to help tell them apart.[4]

In the early days, Madeline and Marion commuted by train between their apartment in New York City and New Rochelle, but during the height of their popularity, Mom moved them to an apartment adjacent to the studio.[5] They were refined young ladies, with a governess and weekly piano lessons. They studied German, history, literature, and French (which they practiced on the train), and enjoyed dancing, boating, and horseback riding when off set. They also seem to have grown up incredibly fast, not unusual for child stars; *Reel Life* claimed they never knew "an unhappy or jarring moment together in their lives,"[6] but that leaves out that by 1914 the girls were separated from their father and brother permanently. Thanhouser scholar Q. David Bowers lists their parents as divorced, but later census records show John as widowed[7] and Jennie as still married (her only union being that with Fairbanks).[8]

One has to strike while the proverbial iron is hot, and stardom's iron cools tragically fast. Jennie had to act quickly, particularly on a chance that could also indulge her own childhood dreams. Between 1914 and 1915, she appeared in eight films for Thanhouser, billed as "Mrs. Fairbanks," and wound up in an episode of *Zudora*, the ambitious yet ill-fated follow-up to *The Million Dollar Mystery*. Jane and the girls teamed up twice, for *The Widow's Mite* (1914) and *$1000 Reward* (1915). She played their mother in both.

Faery stories, comedies, four hankie weepers: the talented teenagers excelled in all genres. Often the films were pitched to a younger audience, over which demographic Thanhouser had the edge. A good example is *Their Great Big Beautiful Doll* (1913), where the twins, upset over the loss of their favorite doll, spy a pretty child (Helen Badgley) in a window and coax her out to play. They take her home, dress her up, and generally make a toy of her, which the toddler loves. It is only when walking her home in the doll carriage that the three learn how their little amusement saved the toddler's life: the house burned down while the

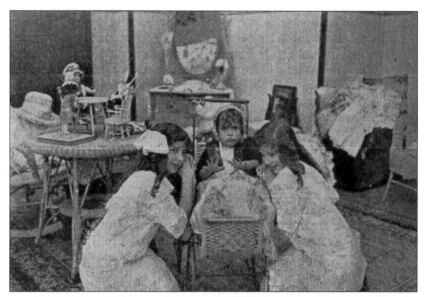

*The twins with Helen Badgley in* Their Great Big Beautiful Doll. *Reel Life,November 22, 1913. Photo courtesy the Media History Digital Library.*

three were away playing together. The child's mother scoops her up with tears of joy, and they all live happily ever after.

Sometimes the typical scripts were abandoned for something more exciting. In *Shep's Race With Death* (1914), the two joined Shep the Thanhouser Collie in a prototypical Lassie-type story, the climax of which has one twin's buggy stuck in the path of an oncoming train. Shep leads the spooked horse off the tracks and saves the day. (Good boy!)

As trapeze performers in *The Flying Twins* (1915), praised for its meticulous recreation of the circus, they earned kudos for their "winsome personalities" and "vivid emotional moments when the Twins hold their own with more mature actresses."[9] They also found their way into two episodes of Thanhouser's greatest triumph, the wildly popular serial *The Million Dollar Mystery*, starring Florence La Badie. Marion and Madeline appeared in over fifty films for the studio between 1912 and 1916, forty of those together, and were "two of the finest little girls that ever grew up."[10]

However, part of growing up is evolving, and they were tired of being one entity. "We have been known so long as the twins in screen productions," Marion remarked to the *New Rochelle Pioneer*, "that now we have reached our fifteenth birthday we think it best that we be known as Marion and Madeline."[11] Both young women were ready to move beyond the constraints of Thanhouser, and by late 1916 they, along with Jennie, were permanently in Manhattan preparing for a return to the stage.

*The Century Girl* was what Ziegfeld did best, a musical revue with a fantastic cast: Leon Errol, Marie Dressler, Hazel Dawn, and Elsie Janis, among others. Madeline and Marion were playing cards—the Jack of Clubs and Jack of Diamonds respectively—in the "Alice in Wonderland" number, with music and lyrics by Irving Berlin. (The King of Hearts was Lilyan Tashman. How apropos.) The show ran for 200 performances, readying the girls for grown-up work indeed: the *Ziegfeld Follies*.

Oh, to have seen the Follies in their heyday! The New Amsterdam sparkled with beautiful ladies wearing Lucile or Erte, rousing musical numbers from Berlin, Kern, Lardner, side-splitting comedy from W. C. Fields and Eddie Cantor, performances by Bert Williams, Ann Pennington, Fanny Brice . . . all staged by the *crème de la crème* of choreographers, Ned Wayburn. His style was a pastiche of tap, ballet, ballroom, gymnastics, and acrobatics. Among other innovations was his "Ziegfeld Walk," the method of descending a staircase in full costume that Vegas showgirls still use today. Old habits die hard; for their 1917 debut they were billed as the Fairbanks Twins. By 1918, they were featured in scenes such as "A Miniature," where they danced a glamorous version of the mirror" routine, later made famous by The Marx Brothers. In the 1919 *Ziegfeld Follies*, they were promoted to "starring" status and featured in "The Follies Salad," where each Follies Girl was dressed as an ingredient. (Marion and Madeline were, of course, Salt and Pepper.)

When Ziegfeld noticed audiences leaving his show only to party into the wee hours at nightclubs, he created the *Midnight Frolic*. It featured talent like Eddie Cantor and Will Rogers, as well as more risqué dance numbers; the girls danced overhead via a glass walkway, and invited patrons to pop their balloon costumes with their cigars. The Fairbanks Twins contributed their

*Madeline (L) and Marion with Eleanor Spalding in* The Flying Twins. Reel Life, *June 26, 1915. Photo courtesy the* Media History Digital Library.

beauty to this, as well as the short-lived *9 O'Clock Frolic*, added to accommodate high-hats with earlier bedtimes. Both ended in 1921, victims of Prohibition. A later attempt to revive the *Midnight Frolic* failed.

Despite the end of their Ziegfeld engagement, 1921 was a banner year for Madeline and Marion. They starred in *Two Little Girls in Blue*, written especially for them and staged by Wayburn. The musical comedy (plot: two sisters can only afford one steamer ticket to India; hijinks ensue) boasted music by Vincent Youmans, later famous for *No No Nanette*, and lyrics by "Arthur Francis,"

*Fairbanks and frippery.* Photoplay, October 1927. *Photo courtesy the* Media History Digital Library.

a.k.a. Ira Gershwin. An ad in *Variety* screamed "TWIN STARS SCINTILLATE ON BROADWAY!"[12]

Their dancing was superb, their singing was . . . nonexistent. Somehow they headlined a musical without being musical. Critics noticed and called them "mute" and "voiceless," yet complimented their "co-

*The twins as Coca and Cola in The Beauty Shop.
Pictures and the Picturegoer, June 1924. Photo
courtesy the Media History Digital Library.*

quettish humor," "exhilirating grace," and "tuneful legs." Alan Dale of the *New York American* applauded their choice not to sing: "Sensible Twins, those Fairbanks sisters! Ladies placed suddenly into musical comedy have often felt that they should sing . . . the Fairbanks duet evidently had wise advisers."[13] Even Dorothy Parker liked their dancing, though she felt it "next to impossible, without straining something beyond repair, to recall a single funny line from [*Blue*]."[14] The success ran for 135 performances at the George M. Cohan Theater.

Built in 1921, The Music Box Theater was built specifically to house Irving Berlin's annual song-and-dance celebration, *The Music Box Revue*. Only four were produced, but the talent that passed through them is legendary. A quick glance reveals William Collier Sr. (stepfather of Buster Collier), The Brox Sisters, Miriam Hopkins, Charlotte Greenwood, Robert Benchley, Frank Tinney, Fanny Brice, and our lovely Madeline and Marion, featured in the 1922-1923 edition. It received good reviews in general, but as for the twins—who actually sang this time—most suggested they shouldn't quit their day job.

While appearing in Berlin's show, Cosmopolitan Productions signed both sisters for a Paramount feature. The "mildly amusing at best"[15] *The Beauty Shop* (1922) starred Raymond Hitchcock (reprising his role from the 1914 stage version) as a "beauty doctor" who, looking to increase prestige, slaps an obscure Italian baron's crest on his products. When the crest is recognized, Dr. Budd, impersonating said baron, travels to Bologna expecting fame and riches. All that awaits him, however, is a vendetta duel, a hideous innkeeper's daughter, and gorgeous twins Coca and Cola. When an attempt to escape with Cola fails, he applies his products to the hideous daughter and poof! She is beautiful now! They all leave for America, the duel forgotten. Louise Fazenda, Billy B. Van, and Montagu Love round out the cast.

1923 was still shaking off the New Years' confetti when the girls announced they were leaving the *Revue*. Vaudeville was calling, and not just any venue: they were booked to premiere at the Palace. According to Vaudeville historian Trav S. D., The Palace was "the perfect showplace for the biggest of big-time Vaudeville . . . [f]or a vaudevillian to have 'played the Palace' was to have died and gone to heaven."[16] This was like going straight from junior varsity football to the Super Bowl, and they knew it. Ned Wayburn and Irving Berlin were again pressed into service, along with song-and-dance man Richard Keene. Marion and Madeline shared the bill with actor-dancer Hal Skelly, later a prolific character actor on TV; screen vamp Valeska Suratt, returning to her singing roots; and blackface comedian Frank Tinney, still a year away from the adultery/domestic violence scandal that would ruin his career. It was a promising lineup, the first one under Keith's new booker[17], and everyone expected brilliance when the curtain rose the week of March 25, 1923. What they got was a flop.

In a misguided attempt to expand their horizons, Madeline and Marion cut back their dancing in exchange for tired, humorless skits and more substandard singing. "They cannot sing," wrote a perplexed *Variety*[18], "and they are hopeless at reading lines." They declared the show a "dismal disappointment" and lamented that the girls even appeared in it. The act limped along at least through May, when an appearance at the Riverside garnered a tepid response.[19]

Drastic times called for drastic measures, and for their next move they did the unthinkable: went their separate ways. Madeline decided to focus on acting, while Marion continued in their

*Marion and Madeline in* On With the Show! Picture Play, *August 1929. Photo courtesy the* Media History Digital Library.

forte, or that was the plan at least; after some stock work, notably *King for a Day* in Chicago, Madeline went right back to musicals, doing *Little Jesse James*, the *Ritz Revue*, and *Mercenary Mary*, among others.

In 1925, during *Mercenary Mary's* run, both twins were injured when a taxi sideswiped the car they were riding in. Marion required seventeen stitches for the lacerations on her hands and arms, and Madeline severely wrenched her back.[20] Thankfully, neither sister had any long-lasting ill effects. Marion toured with the company for George M. Cohan's *Little Nellie Kelly*, then returned for *The Grab Bag* with Ed Wynn, but after three years apart the sisters missed each other terribly. They reunited for the 1926 edition of *George White's Scandals*.[21]

In the audience at *George White's Scandals* was McCormick Steele, self-described broker and Yale football star, class of 1925. He fell hard for Marion (but, strangely, not Madeline) and inundated her with telegrams until she accepted him. The two married in April of 1927[22], while both ladies were appearing in *Oh, Kay!* Three months later, while out with friends, Steele told a police officer he could "wipe up a cellar" with him. He ignored the subsequent summons and was arrested at the Hotel Winthrop, where they lived.  Unable to pay the $15 fine, a messenger was dispatched to gather the funds from Marion. This wasn't Steele's first run-in with the law; he'd received a suspended sentence for disorderly conduct two years earlier.[23]  Marion noticed his true colors early, and reports of separation and divorce floated around the papers as early as 1929, but each time Steele managed to talk her out of it.

When Madeline wasn't trying to convince her sister to leave the bum, she appeared in *Allez-Oop* and *Happy* on Broadway.

The first feature film to use Technicolor, the first feature film with a synchronized soundtrack, the first feature-length all-talking movie happened around this time, and Hollywood was equal parts exhilarated and terrified.  Out of this heady late 20s mélange of color and sound, musical tales of show people and their backstage antics, along with all-star revues of singing and dancing, became all the rage. When current stars collapsed under "triple threat" demands of acting, singing and dancing, studios ransacked Broadway for a whole new crop of actors with voices. Marion and Madeline were tailor-made for the very first to combine everything: the all-dialogue, all-color feature film, *On with the Show!* (1929). As the Dorsey Twins, they "twinkle[d] gayly [sic]"[24] with Joe E Brown, Betty Compson, Sally O'Neil, and Arthur Lake. The film survives today, albeit in only black and white, and while a bit creaky as some early talkies are, it's a lot of fun. (A short Technicolor fragment was found in 2005, along with one from *Gold Diggers of Broadway*.)

By the 1930s, the fabulous Fairbanks fräuleins were winding down. *On with the Show!*, rather than a portent of future work, was their swan song for both stage and screen. In 1932, Marion replaced Eleanor King for a time in *Whistling in the Dark*. The sisters had a cabaret act for a bit in the mid-1930s, even replacing Vivian Vance (a.k.a. Ethel Mertz) at one venue in 1935.[25]

Madeline, married to garment industry executive Leonard Sherman since April 1932[26], testified that year for Marion at her divorce hearing. She and Sherman had found McCormick Steele, still married to Marion, with another woman in their apartment[27]. Despite this, it would still take until December 1939[28] for Marion and Steele to be officially divorced. (Days later, Steele married Myrtle Kraglund, who, as Bobbie Steele, was a celebrated dressage teacher and rider with Ringling Bros. Steele had worked for the circus since 1938[29].)

Marion tried her hand at running a beauty parlor and remarried twice more, both also ending in divorce. She struggled with alcohol in her later years. Madeline, now living in Pennsylvania with Sherman, had one child, a daughter. They divorced in 1947[30], and she moved back to Manhattan the following year. Madeline died of respiratory failure on January 26, 1989. Marion remained in Georgia after settling there with her third and final husband, William Delph. She died there on September 20,

1973, and according to her nephew is interred at the Atlanta cemetery plot of her brother-in-law[31].

1   New York City Deaths, 1892-1902; Deaths Reported in April-May-June, 1892; Certificate #: 12855. Ancestry.com. New York City, Deaths, 1892-1902 [database on-line]. Provo, UT, USA: Ancestry.com Operations Inc, 2003. Accessed February 19, 2015.

2   New York State Archives; Albany, New York; State Population Census Schedules, 1905; Election District: A.D. 31 E.D. 32; City: Manhattan; County: New York; Page:

7. Ancestry.com. New York, State Census, 1905 [database on-line]. Provo, UT, USA: Ancestry.com Operations, Inc., 2014. Accessed February 26, 2015.

3   The *New York Morning Telegraph*, June 23, 1912.

4   "Thanhouser Twinklers Shine Apart." *Motography*, May 20, 1916.

5   New York State Archives; Albany, New York; State Population Census Schedules, 1915; Election District: 04; Assembly District: 02; City: New Rochelle Ward 01; County: Westchester; Page: 05. Ancestry.com. New York, State Census, 1915 [database on-line]. Provo, UT, USA: Ancestry.com Operations, Inc., 2012. Accessed February 25, 2015.

6   *Reel Life*, May 9, 1914

7   Year: 1920; Census Place: Manhattan Assembly District 19, New York, New York; Roll: T625_1221; Page: 10B; Enumeration District: 1330; Image: 298. 1920 United States Federal Census [database on-line]. Provo, UT, USA: Ancestry.com Operations, Inc., 2012. Accessed February 26, 2015.

8   Year: 1940; Census Place: West Palm Beach, Palm Beach, Florida; Roll: T627_606; Page: 62A; Enumeration District: 50-22. 1940 United States Federal Census [database on-line]. Provo, UT, USA: Ancestry.com Operations, Inc., 2012. Accessed February 26, 2015.

9   *Reel Life*, August 14, 1915.

10   Kellette, John William. The *New Rochelle Pioneer*, November 7, 1914.

11   The *New Rochelle Pioneer*, June 3, 1916.

12   Ad in *Variety*, May 27, 1921.

13   Ibid.

14   Parker, Dorothy (2014). *Dorothy Parker: Complete Broadway, 1918-1923*. Ed. Kevin C. Fitzpatrick. Donald Books/iUniverse.

15   *Film Daily*, May 14, 1922.

16   S.D., Trav (2006). *No Applause—Just Throw Money: The Book That Made Vaudeville Famous*. Faber & Faber.

17   *Variety*, February 22, 1923.

18   *Variety*, March 29, 1923.

19   *Variety*, May 17, 1923.

20   "5 Killed, 6 Injured in Day's Auto Toll." *New York Times*, August 16, 1925.

21   "Scandals Cast Completed." *New York Times*, June 3, 1926.

22   "Marion Fairbanks Married." *New York Times*, April 21, 1927.

23   "Actress's Husband Fined." *New York Times*, July 6, 1927.

24   "Fairbanks Twins in 'On With the Show'." *Berkeley Daily Gazette* (CA), September 20, 1929.

25   "Night Club Notes." *New York Times*, February 2, 1935.

26   Year: 1940; Census Place: Hawley, Wayne, Pennsylvania; Roll: T627_3627; Page: 4B; Enumeration District: 64-12. 1940 United States Federal Census [database on-line]. Provo, UT, USA: Ancestry.com Operations, Inc., 2012. Accessed February 26, 2015.

27   "Aids Twin Sister in Suit." *New York Times*, March 15, 1935.

28   "Final Decree Granted in Two Divorce Cases." *Sarasota Herald-Tribune* (FL), December 22, 1939.

29 Year: 1940; Census Place: New York, New York, New York; Roll: T627_2633; Page: 82B; Enumeration District: 31-421. 1940 United States Federal Census [database on-line]. Provo, UT, USA: Ancestry.com Operations, Inc., 2012. Accessed February 26, 2015.

30 *Nevada State Journal* [Reno, NV], August 16, 1947.

31 Hagan, Robert (February 2015). Email interview with author.

## Other Sources:

Bowers, Q. David. *Thanhouser Films: An Encyclopedia and History.* Thanhouser Company Film Preservation, Inc. Web. Accessed February 19, 2015. <http://www. thanhouser.org/tcocd/Navigation_Files/indgag_cs.htm>

"Ernest Truex Et Al." New York Times, May 3, 1925.

*IBDb – The Internet Broadway Database.* Web. Accessed February 21, 2015. <http:// www.ibdb.com/>

"The Jolly Bachelors." *Variety*, January 1910.

Kenrick, John. *Musicals 101 – The Cyber Encyclopedia of Musical Theatre, Film, and Television.* Web. Accessed March 1, 2015. <http://www.musicals101.com/index.html>

"Santa Claus Visits the Blue Family." *New York Times.* December 25, 1910.

"Two Little Girls in Blue." *The Official George and Ira Gershwin Website.* Web. Accessed March 5, 2015. <http://gershwin.com/shows/two-little-girls-in-blue>

# Chapter 6:
# Laura and Violet La Plante

*Laura (L) and Violet La Plante,* Photoplay, *June 1925. Photo courtesy the* Media History Digital Library.

Most of us had a summer job when we were fifteen: mowing lawns, flipping burgers, or doling out one scoop or two at the local beach's snack shack. It meant money in our pockets and maybe a story or two for Friday night. For Laura La Plante, a summer job brought immortality.

Laura Isobel Laplant (she hadn't yet gained the "e") was born in St. Louis, Missouri, on November 1, 1904.[1] She was the first child of Lydia Elizabeth Turk, a schoolteacher from a farming family in Festus, MO, and William Antoin Laplant, from Ste. Genevieve County, MO. William was a jack of all trades: dance teacher, bartender, carpenter, "any type of job he could get" according to Laura. "I think he got tired of places and wanted to move on."[2]

The family never had much money, but the arrival of Violet Virginia Laplant on January 17, 1908[3] pushed them officially into poverty. Fed up with a husband "unhampered by any great sense of responsibility,"[4] Elizabeth sent the girls to live with relatives in California, divorced William, and then joined them. Eventually the three settled down in San Diego, and Elizabeth taught grammar school. When her hearing problems grew too advanced for schoolwork, she took a job in a department store. Elizabeth provided a modest yet secure home for Laura and Violet, even procuring free music lessons for them (Laura violin, Violet cello).

Al Christie first came to California in 1911 and formed Nestor, the first comedy studio in Hollywood. Five years later, he and his brother, Charlie, created their own company; Betty Compson, Syd Chaplin, Marie Prevost, and Marie Dressler all graced their halls. Christie was a comedy powerhouse in the early days of film, on par with anything coming out of Keystone.

Laura's cousin, Mary MacMahon, suggested some extra work while she and Violet visited during summer vacation. "She lived just about a block-and-a-half away, maybe less, from the Christie studio . . . the first job I had there was as a bridesmaid"[5] in a comedy starring Neal Burns and Dorothy Devore. Young Laura had no idea what she was doing, but faked it well enough for a stock contract (and at least $20 a week). She added an "e" to her last name for some Parisian flair. Up through 1920, her most prominent role was as Nora in the *Jiggs* series based on *Bringing Up Father*, a popular comic strip. All that changed the following year, thanks to First National.

"The Old Swimmin' Hole," James Whitcomb Riley's poignant 1883 poem, was a love-letter to childhood at the turn of the last century. *The Old Swimmin' Hole*, the 1921 movie version starring Charles Ray, was equally heartfelt. The plot is almost inconsequential—a snapshot of country boy Ezra Hull's life—but the film itself was experimental: no intertitles were used. It was picturesque, gentle, aimed at audiences "deeply nostalgic for a vanishing America."[6] Supporting Ray were Lincoln Stedman as Ezra's rival; Laura as Myrtle, the girl that breaks Ezra's heart; and Peggy Prevost (sister of Marie, billed as "Marjorie") as the girl whose patient love from afar is rewarded. A misty-eyed *Motion Picture* fawned "you remember the almost-forgotten odor of new-mown hay, fresh earth and honeysuckle . . . [it] is like a tonic."[7] Everyone involved got fine notices: "if any one's disappointed or not pleased . . . then they're more than all wrong." [8] Laura was excited. "I thought that I was sitting on top of the world." Her breakthrough seemed to all but guarantee future A-list projects. However, she smirked, "I hadn't given much thought to the theory that the world is round . . . ."[9]

She fell back into forgettable roles for both 20th Century Fox and Universal. She appeared in several Westerns with Hoot Gibson, as well as Tom Mix and Art Acord, and did some comedy shorts with Neely Edwards. *Perils of the Yukon* (1922), a serial starring William Desmond, required her to do her own stunts; she "never really learned to ride a horse [but] just bluffed it."[10] Laura accepted all roles gladly, even the terrifying ones; her mother's hearing had worsened to the point that work was impossible, and so she was "tickled to death"[11] to have a source of income.

She got a boost in 1923, when she was voted one of the WAMPAS Baby Stars. It was a particularly good year, with Evelyn Brent, Eleanor Boardman, Dorothy Devore, and Jobyna Ralston among the lucky thirteen. Soon after, she made an appearance in *The Thrill Chaser* (1923), another Hoot Gibson comedy about a cowboy heading to Hollywood to break into the movies. It costarred Billie Dove and had a number of cameos including King Baggot, Norman Kerry, Mary Philbin, and Reginald Denny, with whom Laura would be working a prominent amount in the future.

Laura welcomed 1924 with good cheer and a new hair color. "Delighted with an experiment in white henna," wrote Margaret Reid, "she has been a blonde ever since . . . she thinks that blond hair gives her at least a semblance of the dashing person she would like to be."[12] (Kind of snarky, this Ms. Reed.) Dashing Laura also had a lively schedule of several movies simmering, three with Reginald Denny. The best of these was *Sporting Youth* (1924), a car racing comedy. Denny had chosen her specifically as his costar, and Laura adored him: "Reg Denny was a charming, delightful man . . . he was always very helpful when we were working together."[13] Audiences found the onscreen fun infectious, and Universal promoted Laura to leading player. She wasn't just a comedienne, either; she was "very natural and piquant"[14] as a spoiled society girl in the soaper *Butterfly* (1924).

Violet followed in the boot steps of dozens, if not hundreds, of hopeful young ladies, and appeared in a Western as her first

*Violet and Buddy Roosevelt in Battling Buddy.* Exhibitors Trade Review, *June 28, 1924. Photo courtesy the* Media History Digital Library.

picture. *Battling Buddy* (1924) was written for Buddy Roosevelt, a stuntman and actor who worked on *Hell's Hinges* (1916) with William S. Hart and *The Sheik* (1921) with Valentino. Athletic and affable, he had a long and immensely successful career, mostly in B Westerns, through to *The Man Who Shot Liberty Valance* (1962). Critics found Violet (who played the amusingly named Dorothy Parker) "a delightful complement . . . a highly decorative addition to the screen."[15] Concurrently in theatres, she had a small role in Vitagraph's *The Clean Heart* (1924). The film was a critic's darling, "a surprisingly stirring piece of work"[16] with "a real and elusive appeal,"[17] starring Percy Marmont as a disillusioned newspaper writer/editor who flees his life, only to realize his demons have tagged along. Violet finished out the year with three more Westerns, rejoining Buddy Roosevelt for *Walloping Wallace* (1924). She was then added to the cast of "Ann's an Idiot,"[18] based on the tremendously popular novel by Pamela Wynne, and for the first time, Laura and Violet's professional paths crossed.

*Eugene O'Brien and Laura in* Dangerous Innocence. Exhibitors Trade Review, *April 4, 1925. Photo courtesy the* Media History Digital Library.

The adaptation, renamed *Dangerous Innocence* (1925), featured Laura as Ann Church, who falls for much older officer Major Seymour (Eugene O'Brien) during a passage from England to India. The major spurns the girl's affections, not because he lacks interest, but because he had a previous relationship with her mother—one Ann knows nothing about. Not until Ann's virtue is threatened by a leering Gilchrist (Jean Hersholt) does Seymour rush to her aid, confessing his romantic feelings as well as the original reason for hiding them. Violet had an unlisted bit part, as did Janet Gaynor. The entire production team, including director William Seiter, sailed out of Los Angeles in late 1924;[19] in the interest of authenticity, most of the movie was made aboard the Honolulu-bound S.S. *Calawaii.*

Violet was elected a 1925 WAMPAS Baby Star, along with Olive Borden and her cousin Natalie Joyce, June Marlowe, and Madeline Hurlock. *Variety* noted that the year's crop was "weak" and few of the ladies had done anything "on the screen to justify the selection."[20] WAMPAS attempted to raise her cachet by calling her "Violet Avon." *Motion Picture* jumped on board, calling her "the perfect icy blonde—she should play the English aristocrat to perfection."[21] It was a ridiculous move on WAMPAS' part, since Violet had already been publicized as "Violet La Plante, Laura's

*Laura in* Photoplay, *May 1927, and Violet in* Photoplay, *March 1925. Photo courtesy the Media History Digital Library.*

sister" since her film debut. The "Avon" was promptly dropped, and she only appeared in one film that entire year: *The Hurricane Kid* (1925), with Hoot Gibson and Marian Nixon.

Laura's star kept rising with the prestige picture *Smouldering Fires* (1925). The simple love story— girl meets boy, girl loves boy, boy loves girl's sister instead, girl gallantly steps aside—was elevated via a May-December twist. Pauline Frederick exuded regal strength as Jane Vale, forty-year-old factory owner who is not ashamed of having earned a grey hair or two. A young foreman (Malcolm McGregor)'s business acumen gains her respect, and eventually, her love. The two are about to be married when Jane's twenty-year-old sister, Dorothy (Laura), comes to town. It is love at first sight for Robert and Dorothy, and Jane resigns herself to allowing both her loved ones their happiness. Understated acting, particularly from Frederick, kept *Smouldering Fires* from becoming overly melodramatic; her "excellent characterization atones for many of the shortcomings of this production."[22] (I also tend to agree with critic Mordaunt Hall's view in the *New York Times* that Jane was too good for Robert.) Four months after, *Dangerous Innocence* was released; Mordaunt Hall singled out Laura as "quite effective . . . graceful and buoyant."[23] Director Seiter thought so, too; the two had been an item since they'd wrapped on-location shooting. Both he and Laura capped the year with the romantic comedy *The Teaser* (1925).

Old faces came calling in 1926. Violet reteamed with Buddy Roosevelt for *The Ramblin' Galoot* (1926), and Laura reunited with Seiter and Denny for *Skinner's Dress Suit* (1926). Critics didn't expect much of the latter's already tired script: husband lies to wife about a raise refusal and pay cut; wife spends money they don't have, hubby loses it, a pitying universe helps them. A surprise injection of youth and vigor via a Charleston-related subplot saved it. "Laura La Plante and a host of others . . . seem to get keen enjoyment from it—especially the La Plante person." *Motion Picture* felt she should always stick to such light fare instead of "emotional numbers"[24] like *The Midnight Sun* (1926), a turgid Russian melodrama.

The rest of Laura's year was, if not champagne, then soda pop, as bubbly as she was. Director Edward Sloman worked with her on two films that year and found Laura "the nicest, the loveliest, the sweetest girl I've ever worked with."[25] She was a member of Our Club, founded by Mary Pickford. You wouldn't find Clara Bow telling one of her bawdy stories here; Billie Dove, Zasu Pitts, Leatrice Joy, and many others worked hard to present themselves as a wholesome, proper lot. (Alas, Violet was not a member.) November saw Seiter and Laura joined in holy matrimony. "I married Bill Seiter, so I thought he was all right,"[26] she said, never one to mince words. Marriage did little to change her personality. She was still the same unaffected young woman, a bit reticent with strangers but deeply devoted to her loved ones, especially her mother and sister, for whom she had a house built. Her reputation for being "taciturn" and "a mouse-like person" with strangers melted away in front of friends, who saw a warm, friendly woman with "a dry humor more subtle than pointed."[27]

By 1927, Violet drooped. There was her typical annual Western, then a Gladys Brockwell drama the following year. Her last gasp was a small role in *How to Handle Women* (1928), a bizarre film about a country avoiding bankruptcy via a peanut crop; it was an absolute dud. *Photoplay* felt big sis should've pulled strings for Violet, but . . . them's the breaks, kid. Hollywood's a scary place.

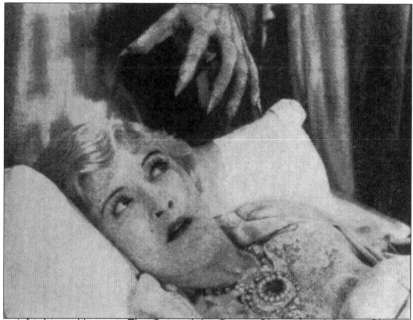

*A frightened Laura in* The Cat and the Canary. Photoplay, *July 1927. Photo courtesy the* Media History Digital Library.

Paul Leni was about to make it scarier. The celebrated director brought the angles and shadows of German expressionism to the granddaddy of all "old dark house" stories, *The Cat and the Canary* (1927). Annabelle West (Laura) will be the sole heir of her eccentric uncle's fortune—provided she spends the night in his moldering mansion. Will she have the intestinal fortitude, or will the abundant spookiness get the upper hand? The "brilliant parody of Gothic horror,"[28] brought to chilling life by Leni and a cast who did "infinitely better work than they have in any other film,"[29] was Laura's cinematic zenith and the film for which she is best remembered today. Smart touches of humor, provided by Creighton Hale and Flora Finch, balanced the somber characterizations of Tully Marshall, Gertrude Astor, and Martha Maddox. "This is a film which ought to be exhibited before many other directors to show them how a story should be told,"[30] raved the *New York Times*, and most agreed. Laura and Leni repeated the formula in *The Last Warning* (1929), another horror-comedy, this time in a haunted Broadway theater. In between the two, she appeared in four films, three of them in 1928, and all of them in her usual formula.

The elder La Plante had the luck to grace a number of cinematic experiments: a film without intertitles, one of the first haunted house thrillers . . . and now she sang onscreen in the first movie version of *Show Boat* (1929). This version, mostly silent, was based on Edna Ferber's book rather than the Broadway musical adaptation, though it did borrow some songs for the sound sequences. Laura, as Magnolia, has two numbers, "Ol' Man River" and "Can't Help Lovin' That Man," but whether or not she was dubbed is unclear. Praise for the picture rested solely on the musical portions, particularly the overture by Paul Whiteman and selections from the Broadway cast. Critics chided director Harry Pollard for his "passion for pathos"[31] and "ponderous" sentimental scenes, but the "captivating melodies" made it worth watching.[32]

Laura appeared in a few other pictures that year, and then eased into the new decade with *Captain of the Guard* (1930) and *King of Jazz* (1930). The latter was Universal's foray into the movie-musical craze, completely in two-strip Technicolor. The title came from Paul Whiteman's self-appointed moniker, and he headlined the "catchy tunes, resplendent costumes and settings and humorous skits"[33] by John Boles, Laura, Jeannette Loff, The Rhythm Boys (led by Bing Crosby), The Brox Sisters, The Sisters G, and many others. (Somewhere in the fray is Delbert Fradenberg, the great-uncle of late Nirvana frontman Kurt Cobain.) It boasted an early appearance by the Russell Markert Girls long before they were the Radio City Rockettes, and the first color cartoon by Walter "Woody Woodpecker" Lantz and William Nolan. Despite Universal's $2 million efforts, *King of Jazz* barely cleared $900,000, thanks to the Depression and a fickle audience already tired of revues. It recouped some money overseas, doing particularly well in South Africa.

While Laura appeared in *King of Jazz*, her final film with the studio, Violet tended to her duties as Vice-President of the Thalians. Young Hollywood, desiring the frivolity of the stars but lacking their bank accounts, started a club that allowed "new players of promise to keep in touch with each other" while meetings at their beach house "provided them with a great deal of pleasure at a small expenditure of cash."[34] Polly Ann and Loretta Young, Sally

*Detail from a Thalians group shot: Claire Windsor (L), Violet, and Edna Murphy.* Picture Play, *August 1930.* Photo courtesy the *Media History Digital Library.*

Blane, Rex Bell, Mary Brian, and Buddy Rogers were just some who danced, swam, or played volleyball at their weekend parties. She abandoned her post in 1931 and headed to Seattle, where she kicked up her heels onstage in *Stepping Sisters*. The comedy about former Burlesque performers, who reunite after twenty years to stage a charity show, was a huge success on Broadway, and the touring production garnered just as many laughs. (It was later made into a popular 1932 film starring Louise Dresser, Minna Gombell, and Jobyna Howland.)

Laura meandered through a number of pleasant yet mediocre comedies: *Lonely Wives* (1931), with her good friend Edward Everett Horton, for Pathé; *God's Gift to Women* (1931), with Frank Fay, a rising Joan Blondell, and a nosediving Louise Brooks, at Warner Brothers; and *Meet the Wife* (1931), with Lew Cody, for Christie. The Masquers' Club, the storied social/charitable organization of film gentlemen, cast her in their first short, *Stout Hearts and Willing Hands* (1931). The RKO-Pathé farce was in homage to the early days of filmmaking, complete with bumbling Keystone Kops. Two other blips on her radar were *Arizona* (1931), with a young John Wayne, (she "remember[ed] nothing about him or the picture"[35]) and the B-movie *The Sea Ghost* (1931).

1932 was unremarkable for both sisters, with Violet's unaccredited part in *Tomorrow and Tomorrow* (1932) and Laura devoid of projects. With her schedule clear, she decided it was the perfect time to travel, so in 1933 she headed for England with a friend. Her husband had no interest in the trip; their marriage was strained, and both parties were ready to move on. Laura met up with producer Irving Asher, who used to give her rides to the studio when they were both eighteen. After the short trip turned into six months, she "called Bill up on the phone from London and said to him, 'I think I'd like to stay here.' . . . He said, 'Okay, stay.' So that's how short and sweet it was."[36] Grounds for divorce was incompatibility. "There is no other reason," she told the press, "and we are still very good friends."[37] Seiter married Marion Nixon, to whom Asher had introduced him, and Laura married Irving Asher in 1934. The four would remain close until Bill's death in 1964. Violet also married in 1934, to chiropractor Charles Benson.

Irving Asher headed the British branch of Warner Bros., at Teddington Studios, and convinced Laura to appear in six films, including another Masquers' short, the Sherlock Holmes parody *Lost in Limehouse* (1933). The best of the six, *Man of the Moment* (1935), was a black comedy starring Douglas Fairbanks Jr. Laura's character attempts suicide but is rescued by Fairbanks, whose fiancée misunderstands and leaves him. The two make a pact: go to Monte Carlo with the honeymoon tickets and hit it big, or else end it all together. It is a marvelous bit of "British screwball," directed by Monty Banks, and a lovely parting note for Laura (so to speak). She left the screen and gave birth to their first child, Jill, in 1936. A second child, Tony, was born in 1939; he went on to co-write several songs with The Beach Boys, including "Wouldn't It Be Nice" and "God Only Knows." When a visit back to the U.S. became permanent due to World War II, Asher joined the Armed

Forces and worked with MGM and Paramount, and Laura devoted herself to raising their two children.

Violet fared more roughly. Her marriage to the philandering Charles was over by 1939, and by 1940 she and her son, Roger, were back living with Elizabeth.[38] According to Hans J. Wollstein, she may have worked as a secretary or receptionist.[39] Violet La Plante died of pneumonia June 1, 1984, aged 76.[40]

Laura's comeback for MGM was in the papers by early 1942 but didn't materialize until *Little Mister Jim* (1947). Both her role and the drama, featuring Jackie "Butch" Jenkins as a child helping his widower father grieve his mother with aid from their Chinese cook, were unexceptional. Laura briefly turned to television, guesting on NBC's comedy *It's A Great Life* in 1955 and playing Belva Lockwood, one of the first women to run for President, in "She Also Ran", a playlet for *Telephone Time* (CBS and ABC) in 1956. Included in the cast were Aileen Pringle and Hal Le Sueur, Joan Crawford's brother. Our last glimpse of the still-lovely Laura was as Betty Hutton's mother in *Spring Reunion* (1957), which critics called "bittersweet but disappointing."[41]

Laura enjoyed life and always viewed her screen career as just another job. "My career was wonderful, but then, so were the years that followed . . . ."[42] She had a happy marriage, sculpted, doted on her grandson, and made the occasional public appearance. She was honored with a street named after her in Agoura Hills,[43] a star on the Hollywood Walk of Fame, and an appearance on *The Night of 100 Stars* in 1985. After Irving's death a month later, Laura lived with Jill. In later years she suffered from a number of illnesses, including Alzheimer's Disease, and relocated to the Motion Picture and TV Hospital. Laura La Plante died of a stroke October 14, 1996, aged 91.[44]

1   Death certificate for Laura La Plante, October 14 1996, File No. 39619043025, County of Los Angeles, CA Board of Health. Scanned and added to Laura La Plante family tree 25 December, 2011, by "ppiotrowski33". Accessed via Ancestry.com March 13, 2015. <http://trees.ancestry.com/tree/36058967/person/188752555887>

2   Drew, Wiliam (1997). *Speaking of Silents: First Ladies of the Screen*. Vestal Press.

3   Death certificate for Violet Benson aka Violet La Plante, June 1 1984, File No. 8009 006607, County of San Diego, CA Board of Health. Scanned and added to Violet La Plante family tree 25 December, 2011, by "ppiotrowski33". Accessed via Ancestry.com March 13, 2015. <http://trees.ancestry.com/tree/36058967/person/188752555888>

4   Reid, Margaret. "Laura – As She Is." *Picture Play*, September 1930.

5   Drew, *Speaking of Silents*.

6   Brownlow, Kevin. "Obituary: Laura La Plante." *The Independent* (UK), October 17, 1996.

7   Fletcher, Adele Whitely. "Across the Silversheet." *Motion Picture*, June 1921.

8   "A Real Picture of Real Life." *Film Daily*, February 20, 1921.

9   St. Johns, Ivan. "Minus the Wand." *Photoplay*, May 1927.

10  Drew, Speaking of Silents.

11  Ibid.

12  Reid, "Laura – As She Is."

13  Drew, *Speaking of Silents*.

14  Pardy, George T. "Registers Strong Emotional Appeal." *Exhibitors Trade Review*, September 13, 1924.

15  Copeland, R.E. "Good Riding Stunt in 'Battling Buddy.'" *Exhibitors Trade Review*, September 20, 1924.

16  "The Screen." *New York Times*, September 15, 1924.

17  "The Shadow Stage." *Photoplay*, December 1924.

18  "Production Highlights." *Exhibitors Trade Review*, December 6, 1924.

19  National Archives and Records Administration (NARA); Washington, D.C.; Passenger Lists of Vessels Arriving at Honolulu, Hawaii, compiled 02/13/1900 - 12/30/1953; National Archives Microfilm Publication:A3422; Roll: 078; Record Group Title: Records of the Immigration and Naturalization Service, 1787 - 2004; Record Group Number: RG 85 [database on-line]. Provo, UT, USA: Ancestry.com Operations, Inc., 2009. Accessed March 12, 2015.

20  "Inside Stuff on Pictures." *Variety*, January 7, 1925.

21  "The Lucky Thirteen on Beauty's Roll of Honor." *Motion Picture*, April 1925.

22  Hall, Mordaunt. "The Screen." *New York Times*, March 31, 1925.

23  Hall, Mordaunt. "The Screen." *New York Times*, June 8, 1925.

24  Reid, Laurence. "The Picture Parade." *Motion Picture*, August 1926.

25  Slide, Anthony (2002). *Silent Players: A Biographical and Autobiographical Study of 100 Silent Film Actors and Actresses*. The University Press of Kentucky.

26  Drew, *Speaking of Silents*.

27  Reid, "Laura – As She Is."

28  Brownlow, "Obit: Laura La Plante."

29  Hall, Mordaunt. "Mr. Leni's Clever Film." *New York Times*, September 18, 1927.

30  Ibid.

31  Hall, Mordaunt. "The Screen." *New York Times*, April 18, 1929.

32  Hall, Mordaunt. "Singing and Talking." *New York Times*, April 21, 1929.

33  "The King of Jazz." *National Board of Review Magazine*, May/June 1930.

34  Mook, Samuel Richard. "Open House for Pep." *Picture Play*, August 1930.

35  Drew, *Speaking of Silents*.

36  Ibid.

37  "Laura La Plante Sues." *New York Times*, March 14, 1934.

38  Year: 1940; Census Place: Los Angeles, Los Angeles, California; Roll: T627_399; Page: 15A; Enumeration District: 60-143. 1940 United States Federal Census [database on-line]. Provo, UT, USA: Ancestry.com Operations, Inc., 2012.

39  Wollstein, Hans J. "Violet La Plante." *All Movie Guide*. Web. Accessed March 9, 2015. <http://www.nytimes.com/movies/person/282028/Violet-LaPlante>

40  Death certificate for Violet Benson aka Violet La Plante (see endnote 3).

41  Weiter, A.H. "Screen: 'Spring Reunion;' Betty Hutton Returns in Film at Palace." *New York Times*, May 6, 1957.

42  Oliver, Myrna. "Laura La Plante; Silent Screen Star Had Girl-Next-Door Image." *Los Angeles Times*, October 16, 1996.

43  Pascal, Susan M., foreword by Sen. Fran Pavley (2013). *Agoura Hills (Images of America)*. Arcadia Publishing.

44  Death certificate for Laura La Plante (see endnote 1).

## Other Sources:

"Al Christie." Hollywood Star Walk. *Los Angeles Times*, n.d. Web. Accessed March 17, 2015. <http://projects.latimes.com/hollywood/star-walk/al-christie/>

Burlingame, Jeff (2006). *Kurt Cobain: Oh Well, Whatever, Nevermind (American Rebels)*. Enslow Publishers.

"Inside Facts on Stage and Screen." *Variety*, May 2, 1931.

Mallory, Mary. "Hollywood Heights: The Masquers Club Laughs to Win." The *Daily Mirror*, 18 August 2014. Web. Accessed March 17, 2015.< http://ladailymirror.com/2014/08/18/mary-mallory-hollywood-heights-the-masquers-club- laughs-to-win/>

McKegg, William H. "Pull Hasn't Helped Them At All." *Photoplay*, August 1928.

Paterno, Vincent. "Hollywood to U.S.: We're Not Evil." *Carole & Co.* Livejournal, 7 July 2009. Web. Accessed March 20, 2015. <http://carole-and-co.livejournal.com/220882.html>

Pereyra, Dennis. "King of Jazz." *The Red Hot Jazz Archive*. Web. Accessed March 20, 2015. <http://redhotjazz.com/kingofjazz.html>

Wollstein, Hans J. "Buddy Roosevelt." *The Old Corral*. Web. Accessed March 20, 2015.< http://b- westerns.com/buddy2.htm>

# Chapter 7:
# Mae and Marguerite Marsh

*Mae Marsh,* Motion Picture, *January 1915, and Marguerite Marsh,* Cine-Mundial, *September 1918. Photos courtesy the* Media History Digital Library.

The remarkable story of the Marshes began in 1887, when May Warne married Stephen Charles Marsh.[1] They had six children: Marguerite (1888), Elizabeth (1890), Oliver (1893), Mae (1895), Frances (1897), and Mildred (1898). It's an oft-repeated story that Stephen Marsh died around 1899, but family legend asserts he deserted his wife and children, leaving May to struggle alone with her young brood. By 1910, she was living in Los Angeles as Mrs. William Hall[2] (no official marriage record exists) in Los Angeles with her "husband"—who, despite reports, did not die in the 1906 earthquake—and five daughters, Marguerite's husband Donald Loveridge, and their daughter Leslie.[3] It was over by 1920, when a single May and the girls, including a divorced Marguerite and Leslie, relocated to Manhattan's West 79th Street.

*Bobby Harron and Mae Marsh in* Man's Genesis. *Motion Picture Story Magazine, August 1912. Photo courtesy the* Media History Digital Library.

Marguerite was the family's first soubrette, performing as Margaret Loveridge with Raymond Hitchcock's company, who voted her "prettiest girl in the chorus."[4] A stint in stock with Morosco followed. Margaret, "of lovely Titian hair and fair of face,"[5] gave little thought to motion pictures. "Hadn't I been on the stage in musical plays and various things—why should I resort to acting by the camera!"[6] Despite her posturing, something intrigued Margaret enough to try. She signed with Biograph in May 1911, her first film the D. W. Griffith-directed faery story *The Blind Princess and the Poet* (1911) with Blanche Sweet. 1912 brought *The Mender of Nets* (1912), with Mabel Normand, and another Sweet picture, *Under Burning Skies* (1912). Margaret was now Marguerite, a daisy of a girl who read "serious looking" books and embroidered between scenes. "I love to sit quietly at home with my books," she remarked. ". . . I am acquiring something that cannot be taken from me."[7] With so many younger siblings, having something of her own was precious indeed. She was no wet blanket, however: "Lovey," as her friends called her, had "plenty of good times—all any girl needs to have!"[8] Astrology was her number one passion. She studied, attended classes, and drew up charts for anyone who asked. (I wonder if she made one for Mae?)

Tales of Mae Marsh's beginnings were as abundant as her freckles. The slight, awkward girl visited her sister's set and was largely ignored—by everyone but Griffith. "The frail, appealing look of her struck him,"[9] remembered Griffith's wife, Linda Arvidson. Lillian Gish noted Mae's humble response when Griffith approached her for picture work: "I don't think there's any chance."[10] The director thought otherwise and put her in *A Siren of Impulse* (1912), his mind's eye already envisioning her "bringing home the cows or portraying some other old-fashioned heroine . . ."[11] Mae kept doing bit parts, often with her sister; the pair appeared in eight films together, five that first year alone. In between, she recalled how Griffith groomed her for the art of movie acting, "teaching me how, when, and where to place my feet and how to move my body. . . ."[12]

Mae's big break was *Man's Genesis* (1912), a role turned down by both Blanche Sweet and Mary Pickford because of the skimpy wardrobe. Mae was "Lilywhite," a grass-clad cavewoman opposite Robert Harron's "Weakhands," in a "physiological theory of the birth of the stone hammer . . . ."[13] The capable prehistoric drama also gave audiences the first glimpse of Bobby and Mae's marvelous chemistry together, which continued in the greatly successful romance *The Sands of Dee* (1912). Mae remained in California when Biograph returned to home base in New York, but before long Griffith personally sent two tickets for Mae and her mother to join them. "Everyone adored her," recalled Gish. "Her days as an ugly duckling were over."[14] Griffith was shocked when she arrived not with Mama but instead a hopeful Marguerite in tow. The director only had eyes for Mae; after Pickford left to form United Artists with Douglas Fairbanks and Charlie Chaplin, Griffith knew her delicate poignancy was the perfect replacement. Marguerite worked, but found herself considered "Mae's sister" for the remainder of her career.

*Marguerite when she was still Margaret Loveridge.* Moving Picture World, *April 12, 1913. Photo courtesy the Media History Digital Library.*

1913 brought upheaval to the close-knit film family. Mae and the others were frantically busy with the rapid-fire one and two-reelers that were their bread and butter, but Griffith was frustrated and stifled. He knew multi-reel "features" were the future, and poured his vision into the four-reel Biblical drama, *Judith of Bethulia.* Blanche Sweet and Henry Walthall played the leads, Mae and Bobby supported, and the Gish sisters, Kate Bruce, and Harry Carey were featured. Biograph's squabbling over time and expense not only shelved the picture but hastened Griffith's departure; by the time Biograph released *Judith of Bethulia* to critical acclaim in 1914, Griffith and his company of actors, directors, and crew members were comfortably settled at Reliance-Majestic. Mae blossomed into a star there, in films such as *The Escape* (1914) and *The Avenging Conscience* (1914).

One of Mae's most fondly remembered of the period, *Home Sweet Home* (1914) featured H. B. Warner as John Payne, composer of the title song, whose one effort in a life of meager accomplishment had a lasting influence on future listeners. The first, a young miner called The Eastener (Bobby Harron), was in love with Apple Pie Mary of the local lunch counter (Mae Marsh). When he decides to abandon Apple Pie Mary for another woman (Miriam Cooper) back home, the strains of "Home Sweet Home" from a passing organ grinder change his mind and send him back into Mary's arms. Additional vignettes included a woman stopped from committing adultery and a grieving mother saved from suicide, both through chance hearing of the song. Other Griffith favorites in the cast were the Gish sisters, Donald Crisp, Blanche Sweet, and James Kirkwood. Mae's segment was the best received, and the actress had "the greatest chance to distinguish herself."[15] Reviews were mostly positive, but some felt less heavy-handed storytelling would've improved things greatly.

Marguerite spent 1914 hard at work, most often in Apollo Comedies (a division of Majestic) opposite former Biograph alum Fred Mace. That autumn she appeared in five films at Thanhouser, including the tense kidnapping drama *Pawns of Fate* (1914), where she rescued the Fairbanks Twins. When Fred Mace started his own company, Flamingo Film, he gave Marguerite the lead in its inaugural offering *Without Hope* (1914). Amateur author Elaine Stern's prize-winning script was a convoluted farce of inventions, spies, hidden identities, and unrequited love. *Without Hope* got good grades for Mace's directorial work but not much else. "What was expected to be a 'knockout' was a disappointment," complained *Variety*. "The principals seemed unable to put the picture over . . . [t]he Flamingo Co. will have to try again."[16] They did, but after the comedy *A Puritan Conscience* (1915), they were defunct.

*The Birth of a Nation* (1915) is challenging to watch for some people today. The sting of its blatant racism has only worsened one hundred years after the initial release. There are several good reasons to see it, however: its initial release polarized the entire country and was a seminal moment in United States race relations; it was a passionately crafted cinematic experience, the prototype

of the blockbuster; and the all-star cast boiled over with outstanding performances.

Mae stunned audiences as Flora, The Pet Sister of Henry B. Walthall's Little Colonel, choosing death over sexual assault by Gus, the "renegade Negro" (Walter Long in blackface). Griffith once told Mae he didn't want actresses, he wanted "people to think what they're doing . . . the expression on your face will be right."[17] Mae excelled at this. "I know I completely forgot I was Mae Marsh," she admitted, "and just became the hunted one in reality."[18] Her natural, subdued acting was a

*Bobby Harron and Mae in* Intolerance. Motion Picture News, *September 23, 1916. Photo courtesy the* Media History Digital Library.

sea change from traditional stage melodrama; Lillian Gish, herself no slouch, felt "she had a quality of pathos in her acting that has never been equaled."[19] The happy innocent jarred by tragedy or trauma into adulthood became Mae's trademark. *The Birth of a Nation* played to packed houses for years, inciting admiration and anger, respect and riots, and the lessons Griffith learned paved the way for his next *tour de force*.

*Intolerance* (1916) is the most likely introduction to Griffith's brilliance for modern audiences. Chastened by *The Birth of a Nation*, he devised four separate scenarios tracing the detrimental effect of bigotry through history: the fall of Babylon, Christ's crucifixion, the slaughter of the Huguenots, and the modern working-class. An exhaustive cast of over seventy included the usual Griffith favorites (the Gishes *et al*) as well as Constance Talmadge, Bessie Love, Elmo Lincoln, and George Walsh. Marguerite even earned a spot as a debutante. Detailed costumes and historically accurate sets brought uncanny authenticity:

Lillian Gish marveled at the "immense, opulent Babylonian set" complete with hanging gardens and 200-foot walls, the "cobble-stoned streets of sixteenth-century Paris," and the Medici court resplendent with "magnificent wall tapestries [and] a canopy of the most intricate mosaics."[20]

Mae and Harron headlined the modern story, originally planned as a stand-alone picture entitled *The Mother and the Law*. The Boy (Harron), a factory worker, strikes with his coworkers after learning their wages were slashed and donated to a dubious charity. The same charity takes possession of his and the Dear One (Marsh)'s child after he is framed by a gangster and sent to prison. Upon his release, The Boy finds the Dear One struggling with the gangster, who is suddenly shot dead by the gangster's own mistress, spying from the hedges. The Boy is arrested for murder and the Dear One fights desperately to exonerate him before his execution. "The observer would prove himself quite lax were he to make no note of Mae Marsh's acting,"[21] praised *Motography*. The Dear One's desperation, grief, and terror in the courtroom deeply affected picturegoers, and time did not lessen the impact: Blanche Sweet recalled a woman crying out during the same scenes when shown at the Museum of Modern Art in 1976.[22] "Miss Marsh set a new standard for the greatest of the actresses who are to come to the screen . . . ."[23]

1916 introduced Triangle, the film studio founded by Griffith, Mack Sennett, and Thomas Ince. Mae was featured in "[e]xpertly made 'little' pictures,"[24] charming romances and dramas that exponentially increased her popularity. The best of these was *Hoodoo Ann* (1916), written by Griffith (under the pseudonym Granville Warwick), with titles by Anita Loos and a "high degree of suspense . . . heart interest and humor."[25] Ann, a luckless orphan, gets a rotten palm reading from the cook: she will be cursed until she marries. She is adopted and a possible solution appears in the form of Jimmie, the boy next door (Harron, of course), but an accident frightens Ann into believing she's killed her neighbor and that Jimmie will never marry her now. Everything comes out in the wash, the neighbor is fine, and Ann and Jimmie get their happy ending . . . but does the curse really go away?

*From L to R: Leslie Marsh, Dorothy Gish, and Mildred Marsh in* Remodeling Her Husband. Photoplay, *September 1920. Photo courtesy the* Media History Digital Library.

Marguerite's achievements in 1915 were infinitely removed from her sister's, but two deserve mention. *The Doll House Mystery* (1915) was one of the Reliance-Majestic one and two-reelers that Griffith delegated to other directors. Though the amount of personal involvement he had in those projects varied, they bear enough of the Griffith stamp to prove his protégés were well-versed in his style. This two-reel suspense story starring Marguerite as a socialite's wife boasted strong camera expertise and character development. "Mediocre . . . at best"[26] was the 15-chapter *Runaway June* (1915), starring Norma Phillips as a runaway bride, which gained some momentum thanks to a nationwide contest; the grand prize was a trip to the Panama-Pacific and San Diego Expositions. After her appearance in *Intolerance*, Marguerite appeared in seven more pictures, including *Casey at the Bat* (1916) with DeWolf Hopper, the anti-drug *The Devil's Needle* (1916) with Tully Marshall and Norma Talmadge, and the Douglas Fairbanks adventure *The Americano* (1916), his last film for Triangle. Baby sister Mildred also went before the camera, with small parts in the "absorbing two-part drama of domestic life"[27] *Hearts United* (1915) and the Francesca Billington drama *The Kinship of Courage* (1915), both for Reliance-Majestic.

Fame turns a person into a commodity, and inevitably, other companies eagerly dangle their carrots and cross their fingers. Goldwyn offered Mae an almost unheard-of $2,500 per week; ever loyal, she asked Griffith's advice, who kindly told her to not throw such money away. Mae reluctantly became a "Goldwyn Girl,"[28] and while the money may have been better, the projects weren't. None of her fourteen films there emphasized her quiet vulnerability the way Griffith had, resulting in "maudlin and cloy- ing"[29] roles and greatly diminished star power by 1919, but by then Mae didn't mind. She had married Goldwyn's first-ever publicity agent, Louis Lee Arms, the year before, and her current thoughts were more diapers than dialogue. (They eventually had a son and two daughters.) After a few more films, both here and overseas, she retired and became a stay-at-home mom.

Marguerite averaged about five movies a year between 1918 and 1919. Her efforts were seldom rewarded with anything kinder than "not out of the ordinary,"[30] but one opportunity was extraordinary indeed: Rolfe's 15-chapter serial *The Master Mystery* (1919). Quen- tin Locke (Harry Houdini), an agent for the Justice Department, battled an evil cartel bent on destruction via biological weap- onry and a powerful robot. Marguerite was Eva Brent, Locke's love interest. Each chapter ended with a life-threatening trap for Locke to escape (spoiler: he did). *The Master Mystery* did formi- dable business, mostly because it offered the unique chance to see both an exciting mystery picture and a performance from the greatest escape artist of all time.

After The Master Mystery ended, she appeared in *The Carter Case* (1919), a serial crime drama starring Herbert Rawlinson and Ethel Grey Terry. Later came small roles alongside Madge Bellamy, Lionel Barrymore, Dustin Farnum, and the lead in *Face to Face* (1922), the only picture from Reginald Warde Productions. Her last film was *The Lion's Mouse* (1923), another crime drama, for Britain's Granger Films / Netherlands-based Hollandia. Marguerite Marsh

*Harry Houdini and Marguerite Marsh in an episode of* The Master Mystery. The Photo-Play Journal, *March 1919. Photo courtesy the Media History Digital Library.*

died of pneumonia on December 8, 1925, aged 37.[31] She was survived by her daughter Leslie, who as Leslie Loveridge joined Aunt Mae in *The Battle at Elderbrush Gulch* (1913), and as Leslie Marsh acted alongside Aunt Mildred in *Remodeling Her Husband* (1920).

Griffith was able to coax Mae back to the screen for *The White Rose* (1923) opposite Ivor Novello. The last of her great silent roles, she played the naïve Teazie, seduced, pregnant, and abandoned by Novello, secretly a minister on self-appointed sabbatical. After the child's birth, the "flighty little cigaret [sic] girl"[32] refuses to name the father and suffers the indignities of being fired and evicted. She makes her way to the Louisiana bayou, filled with "poignancy and beauty,"[33] where after the requisite Griffith miseries she finds happily ever after (with the minister, of course). A few other lesser films, and a trip to England to film Novello's *The Rat* (1925), and she slipped happily back into retirement.

The Depression had other plans. In need of money after the Crash, Mae took the role of Ma Shelby in 20th Century Fox's remake of *Over the Hill* (1932). Audiences wept at her long-suffering

*Mae, Sally Eilers, and James Dunn in* Over the Hill. *Screenland, February 1932. Photo courtesy the* Media History Digital Library.

mother who, despite having lived almost solely for her three children, seems destined for the poorhouse thanks to their selfish
ingratitude . . . until one penitently steps up. *Screenland* dared
readers to "watch Mae Marsh as the little mother without fighting down that lump in your throat . . . ."[34] *Over the Hill* was the
sentimental subject matter in which Mae outclassed all others,
and ushered in a new era for her: the often uncredited character/
cameo actress. From *That's My Boy* (1932) to *Cheyenne Autumn*
(1964), she enhanced over ninety film and TV productions, many
of them classics, such as *The Grapes of Wrath* (1940), *How Green
Was My Valley* (1941), *The Song of Bernadette* (1943), *A Tree
Grows in Brooklyn* (1945), *Miracle on 34th Street* (1947), and *The
Quiet Man* (1952). She was a favorite of John Ford and appeared
in almost all of his work through 1964, when she retired for good.

In 1955 Mae was honored, along with Lillian Gish, Mary Pickford,
Gloria Swanson, and Norma Talmadge, for "distinctive contribu-
tions to the American cinema"[35] by the George Eastman House.
Honored with them were Chaplin, Keaton, Lloyd, Richard Barthelmess, Ronald Colman, and a collection of prominent directors and cameramen. She also received a star on the Hollywood
Walk of Fame. Her golden years were spent blissfully in Hermo-
sa Beach, California, with husband Louis. "We managed to get

through it all . . . and never fell out of love," he remarked shortly before his death. "Why she chose me I don't know. She was the biggest movie star in the world."[36] Mae Marsh died of a heart attack at her home on February 13, 1968, at age 72.[37] Louis died twenty years later at the age of 101.

Frances Marsh climbed the ladder from script clerk to respected film editor on films such as *Design for Living* (1933) and *The Merry Widow* (1934). She died in 1958.[38]

Oliver Marsh started as a cameraman in the mid-1910s and became one of the most sought-after cinematographers at MGM. He earned a special Academy Award for *Sweethearts* (1938) and was Jeannette MacDonald's exclusive cameraman. Oliver's son Owen became a camera operator, and son Werne was a noted jazz saxophonist. Oliver died in 1941.[39]

Mildred played in a total of five films, her last being *The Country Flapper* (1922). Her first marriage made headlines when actress Hazel Howell was named as co-respondent[40] in the 1931 divorce. She died in 1975.[41]

Elizabeth, the sole sibling who did not work in the film industry, married into it. She had three children with husband George Berthelon, Cecil B. DeMille's production manager. She died in 1932.[42]

1  "Kansas Marriages, 1840-1935," database, FamilySearch (https://familysearch.org ark:/61903/1:1:FW2R-WX9 : accessed August 29 2015), Stephen C. Marsh and Mae T. Warne, 08 Jun 1887; citing Douglas, Kansas, reference ; FHL microfilm 1,547,790.

2  "United States Census, 1910", database with images, FamilySearch (https://familysearch.org/ark:/61903/1:1:MVLQ-DL6 : accessed August 29 2015), William Hall, 1910.

3  "New York, New York City Births, 1846-1909," database, FamilySearch (https://familysearch.org/ark:/61903/1:1:2WCC-79P : accessed August 29 2015), Leslie Hall Loveridge, 07 Nov 1907; citing Birth, Manhattan, New York, New York, United States, New York Municipal Archives, New York; FHL microfilm 1,991,836.

4  "A Raymond Hitchcock Party." *New York Times*, January 3, 1910.

5  Griffith, Mrs. D.W. (Linda Arvidson) (1925). *When the Movies Were Young*. E.P. Dutton & Company.

6  Montayne, Lillian. "The Hobbies of Marguerite." *Photo-play Journal*, February 1919.

7  Ibid.

8  Ibid.

9  Griffith, *When the Movies Were Young*.

10   Gish, Lillian, with Ann Pinchot (1969). *The Movies, Mr. Griffith, and Me*. Prentice-Hall, Inc.

11   Griffith, *When the Movies Were Young*.

12   "The Girl on the Film: 'Pictures' Interviews Mae Marsh." *Pictures and the Picture-goer*, December 4, 1915.

13   "Man's Genesis." *Moving Picture World*, July 17, 1915.

14   Gish and Pinchot, *The Movies, Mr. Griffith, and Me*.

15   Michell, A. Danson. "Home Sweet Home." *Motion Picture News*, June 6, 1914.

16   "Without Hope." *Variety*, January 9, 1915.

17   Schickel, Richard (1984). *D.W. Griffith: An American Life*. Simon & Schuster.

18   "The Girl on the Film," *Pictures and the Picturegoer*.

19   Gish and Pinchot, *The Movies, Mr. Griffith, and Me*.

20   Ibid.

21   Kennedy, Thomas C. "Current Releases Reviewed: 'Intolerance.'" *Motography*, September 23, 1916.

22   Slide, Anthony (2002). *Silent Players: A Biographical and Autobiographical Study of 100 Silent Film Actors and Actresses*. The University Press of Kentucky.

23   Kennedy, "Current Releases Reviewed: 'Intolerance.'"

24   Franklin, Joe, William K. Everson (1959). *Classics of the Silent Screen: A Pictorial Treasury*. Citadel Press/Bramhall House.

25   Cooper, Oscar. "Hoodoo Ann." *Motion Picture News*, April 15, 1916.

26   Rainey, Buck (2010). *Serial and Series: A World Filmography, 1912-1956*. 3rd ed. McFarland.

27   photo caption in Reel Life, June 5, 1915, cover.

28   "New Goldwyn Release Sheet Contains Varied Offerings." The *Dramatic Mirror*, January 19, 1918.

29   Franklin and Everson, *Classics of the Silent Screen*.

30   Fred. "The Phantom Honeymoon." *Variety*, November 21, 1919.

31   "New York, New York City Municipal Deaths, 1795-1949," database, FamilySearch (https://familysearch.org/ark:/61903/1:1:2W1D-PZ8 : accessed August 29 2015), Marguerite C. Marsh, 08 Dec 1925; citing Death, Manhattan, New York, New York, United States, New York Municipal Archives, New York; FHL microfilm 2,047,292.

32   Fletcher, Adele Whitely. "Across the Silversheet." *Motion Picture*, August 1923.

33   Ibid.

34   Evans, Delight. "Reviews of the Best Pictures: 'Over the Hill.'" *Screenland*, February 1932.

35   "Film Pioneers Honored." *New York Times*, November 3, 1955.

36   Bogert, John. "Silent film star makes a lasting impression." *Daily Breeze*, November 15, 2010. Web. Accessed August 29, 2015. <http://www.dailybreeze.com/general-news/20101115/john-bogert-silent-film-star-makes-a-lasting-impression>

37   "Mae Marsh, Sister in 'Birth of a Nation,' Is Dead." *New York Times*, February 14, 1968.

38   Date: 1958-03-03, Ancestry.com. California, Death Index, 1940-1997 [database on-line]. Provo, UT, USA: Ancestry.com Operations Inc, 2000. State of California.

California Death Index, 1940-1997. Sacramento, CA, USA: State of California Department of Health Services, Center for Health Statistics.

39   Date: 1941-05-05, Ancestry.com. California, Death Index, 1940-1997 [database on-line]. Provo, UT, USA: Ancestry.com Operations Inc, 2000. State of California. California Death Index, 1940-1997. Sacramento, CA, USA: State of California Department of Health Services, Center for Health Statistics.

40   "Screen Vampire Is Named By Mae Marsh's Sister." *Pittsburg Post-Gazette*, May 2, 1931.

41   Date: 1975-07-14, Ancestry.com. California, Death Index, 1940-1997 [database on-line]. Provo, UT, USA: Ancestry.com Operations Inc, 2000. State of California. California Death Index, 1940-1997. Sacramento, CA, USA: State of California Department of Health Services, Center for Health Statistics.

42   Ancestry.com. California, Death Index, 1905-1939 [database on-line]. Provo, UT, USA: Ancestry.com Operations, Inc., 2013. California Department of Health and Welfare. California Vital Records-Vitalsearch (www.vitalsearch- worldwide.com). The Vitalsearch Company Worldwide, Inc., Pleasanton, California.

## Other Sources:

Bowers, Q. David (1995). "Loveridge, Marguerite a.k.a. Marguerite Marsh." *Thanhouser Films: An Encyclopedia and History*. Thanhouser Company Film Preservation, Inc. Web. Accessed August 12, 2015. <http://www.thanhouser.org/tcocd/Biography_Files/idh6_h62z.htm>

"California, County Marriages, 1850-1952," database with images, FamilySearch (https://familysearch.org/ark:/61903/1:1:XLHZ-SM5 : accessed August 29 2015), Donald M Loveridge and Marguerite C Marsh, 02 Mar 1907; citing Los Angeles, California, United States, county courthouses, California; FHL microfilm 1,033,245.

"California, County Marriages, 1850-1952," database with images, FamilySearch (https://familysearch.org/ark:/61903/1:1:XLWL-PHV : accessed August 29 2015), George Bertholon and Elizabeth Marsh, 23 Feb 1909; citing Los Angeles, California, United States, county courthouses, California; FHL microfilm 1,033,215.

Chamberlain, Safford, Gary Foster (Foreword) (2004). *An Unsung Cat: The Life and Music of Warne Marsh (Studies in Jazz)*. Scarecrow Press.

Everson, William K. (1978). *American Silent Film*. Oxford University Press.

"Marsh and Company." *Photoplay*, September 1920.

"The Master Mystery." *Variety*, November 15, 1918.

Mark. "The Birth of a Nation." *Variety*, March 12, 1915.

Stone, Tammy. "The Silent Collection – Featuring: Mae Marsh." *Immortal Ephemera*. n.d. Web. Accessed August 5, 2015. <http://www.things-and-other-stuff.com/movies/profiles/mae-marsh.html>

# Chapter 8:
# Ella, Ida Mae, and Fay McKenzie

From L to R: *Ella*, Exhibitors Herald and Moving Picture World, *June 16, 1928.*
*Ida Mae*, Picture Play August 1921. *Fay*, Exhibitors Trade Review, *December 16,*
*1922. Photos courtesy the* Media History Digital Library.

The McKenzie girls were never destined to be switchboard operators: greasepaint was in their blood. Their father Robert was a seasoned pro on the stage, touring with stock productions for years. He was a "barrel-chested, snaggle-toothed"[1] fellow, gregarious and hard-working; "[h]e was darling [and] absolutely loved by all," remembered Fay. "He was a fast study; could do anything."[2]

Eva, their mother, sang and danced as a small child with her sister and brother in The Heazlit Trio, whom critics called "three clever children"[3] and "certainly very talented."[4] She continued acting on the stage after their Vaudeville act folded.

Bob and Eva were thrilled to take the plunge into motion pictures with Essanay in 1915, and even more excited to get daughters Ella and Ida Mae, both born in 1911,[5] into the business. Studio co-founder G. M. Anderson, who entered motion picture work in *The Great Train Robbery* (1903), put the couple immediately to work in an inexhaustible supply of Western shorts, most written, directed by and starring Anderson, who had since gained prominence as Broncho Billy. Occasionally one or both girls joined Mom and Pop onscreen in the tremendously popular *Broncho Billy* franchise or the *Snakeville* comedy series. They rubbed elbows with Chaplin and Ben Turpin until January 1916, when Bob moved the gang to Los Angeles.[6]

Their pace never slackened once they hit Hollywood. Bob cranked out unbilled appearances in everything from features with Laura La Plante and Norman Kerry to Westerns and short subjects alongside Charles Chaplin and Harry Carey. Eva and the girls were featured in comedies, Ida Mae in particular sharing a series of shorts with chimp star "Snooky the Humanzee" for Chester. "She has neither the looks nor the air of an actress child," said journalist Emma-Lindsay Squier. "[She] has aspirations to be a writer."[7] Ella's plump physique served her well with Educational and Christie, in cringe-worthy roles like "chubby neighborhood child" or "crying fat girl." Both sisters supported child star Buddy Messinger in some of his Century comedies,[8] [9] and continued to share credits with one or both parents in two-reelers or Westerns.

Ella and Ida Mae were sometimes billed together as the Mckenzie Twins, but this was a bit of creative subterfuge. After Eva's younger sister Ella died of scarlet fever,[10] Bob and Eva took in her one- month old daughter. Since their own daughter and Ella's child were both only four months apart, they decided to raise them as twins. Ida Mae, who didn't know she was adopted until she was fifteen, felt this was the answer to why her parents favored her sister/cousin. (Years later, Ella admitted she felt her parents always favored the adopted Ida Mae.[11]) The "twins" were often a film's bright spot; in *Jane Goes A-Wooing* (1919) starring Vivian Martin, their performances were called "some of the few really human incidents in the picture."[12]

Eunice (who went by her middle name Fay) was born in 1918, and made her film debut at ten weeks, carried by the inimitable Gloria Swanson in *Station Content* (1918). Her first actual acting job came three years later in *A Knight of the West* (1921), a family production: Mom wrote and Dad directed the comedy/Western. "One of the best things the producers did was to place little Fay

McKenzie in the cast," praised one review. "[T]his three-year-old youngster's work is really extraordinary."[13] It was the first film for WBM Photoplays, specializing in ultra-low budget Westerns (and partly a McKenzie company.) Fay also appeared in *Judgment of the Storm* (1924), playing twins with Frankie Darro, and in *Irene* (1926) with the "flaming youth" herself, Colleen Moore.

The McKenzie clan lived in Beverly Hills as the Crash gave way to the Depression.[14] Mom and Pop's eclectic résumé grew exponentially: Charley Chase, Gene Autry, W.C. Fields, Harry Langdon, and The Three Stooges all counted them in their casts. Bob kept his Tent Theatre running, staging full-scale productions (*Uncle Tom's Cabin* featured a "full chorus of cotton pickers . . . render[ing] tuneful spirituals") for "family clientele."[15] Eva found her way into the Lubitsch masterpiece *Trouble in Paradise* (1932), and, at the other end of the spectrum, the drug exploitation film, *The Pace That Kills* (1935). Ida Mae dropped off the Hollywood map after an unaccredited appearance in DeMille's *The Godless Girl* (1929).

A grown-up (and slimmed down) Ella appeared in Paul Leni's *Phantom*-esque *The Last Warning* (1929), the final film in his horror-thriller trilogy for Universal (the other two being *The Cat and the Canary* (1927) and *The Man Who Laughs* (1928)), and a new RKO contract placed her in films such as *Alice Adams* and *Sylvia Scarlett* (both 1935) with Katharine Hepburn. A mini-family reunion of sorts on *The Mysterious Avenger* (1936): Robert, Eva, and Ella all appeared in this routine Western for Columbia about cattle rustlers, featuring a musical interlude by Roy Rogers (as a member of the "Sons of the Pioneers").

Ella followed it with a small role in The Three Stooges short, *Dizzy Doctors* (1937),[16] then retired a few months later after marrying comedian and sneezer extraordinaire Billy Gilbert. Gilbert and Ella were a perfect match: born to opera singers, he'd lived essentially the same life as the McKenzies, working in Vaudeville since age twelve and starting in films as a gag writer for Hal Roach (recommended by Stan Laurel, no less). Today, he is best known for his work with Laurel and Hardy, especially the Oscar-winning *The Music Box* (1932), and as the voice of (who else?) Sneezy in *Snow White and the Seven Dwarfs* (1937).

Ella and Billy on the happy day. Hollywood, January 1938. Photo
courtesy the Media History Digital Library.

Ella saw Billy on the set one day and it was love at first sight.
According to Leonard Maltin, "Billy . . . didn't want any part of her
but . . . [s]he finally did win out and he hasn't regretted it for a day
since."[17] They were wed in the home of director W.S. Van Dyke,[18]
with Charley Chase as best man. Many in Hollywood circles, like

Rudy Vallee and Jimmy Durante, were loyal longtime friends, and Billy and Ella were loved a great deal for their "warm feeling of love, devotion, and . . . true enjoyment of life."[19]

The breakout McKenzie, without a doubt, was Fay. After a ten-year hiatus ("I had to go to school!"[20]), she returned in the musical *Student Tour* (1934), with Jimmy Durante, Nelson Eddy, Charles Butterworth, and her classmate from MGM's Little Red School-house, Betty Grable. From there it was steady work in bargain-basement oaters with Buddy Roosevelt and Wally Wales; lobby cards show her impossibly childlike, playing the female lead at only fifteen. The classic *Gunga Din* (1939) made its way onto her roster, but her work in it was fleeting at best. She briefly became Fay Shannon, thinking an Irish-sounding last name might help her chances during initial *Gone with the Wind* casting. (It didn't.) The new name lasted only one picture, *Ghost Town Riders* (1938). She also followed in Eva's footsteps with a small role in the exploitation films, *Assassins of Youth* (1937) and *Mad Youth* (1940).

Bob showed no signs of slowing down in the 1940s, tucking more Western credits under his ample belt. He and Eva reunited with The Three Stooges, playing Ma and Pa in *The Yoke's On Me* (1944).[21] For them both, it was one of their last credits. Eva retired after the Fibber McGee and Molly movie *Heavenly Days* (1944), and Bob's last credit was *Duel in the Sun* (1946) with Gregory Peck. True to form, he remained active in theater, and it was while re-hearsing for a play in Rhode Island that he died of a heart attack in 1949.[22] (Eva died in 1967.[23])

Fay started the decade with small uncredited roles: waitress, party guest, or background color in films such as *It's a Date* (1940) with Deanna Durbin and *Ma! He's Making Eyes at Me* (also 1940) with Tom Brown. An excited Fay costarred with Ken Maynard in *Death Rides the Range* (filmed in 1939 but released in 1940), but stopped short of being starstruck: "[He] seemed to me to be a little long in the tooth at the time . . . maybe I shouldn't say that."[24] She had a credited role in *When the Daltons Rode* (1940), a Universal Western starring Randolph Scott and Kay Francis, but it wasn't until Republic that she found her niche—and it was all thanks to Ella.

*Fay and Gene Autry in* Down Mexico Way. Cine-Mundial, *August 1942. Photo courtesy the* Media History Digital Library.

Fay had just returned to Hollywood after a Broadway stint in the musical *Meet the People* (1940-41) when Ella arranged a meeting between her and Republic president Herbert J. Yates. "My sister said to wear just a bathing suit, draped by the pool. Yates met me, I was asked to come down to the studios the next day and test. . . . "[25] She was instantly signed to the first of five Gene Autry films, *Down Mexico Way* (1941). It was a colossal hit and Fay achieved stardom at last.

Audiences fell instantly in love—or perhaps something a little naughtier—with her: "[s]he is electric. She is exciting. She is put together like a roller coaster."[26] Sure, she was "The Girl with the Blitzkrieg Eyes" and "The Camera Appeal Girl" (photogenic on all four sides!) but the bubbly twenty-two-year- old "could do more

*A radiant Fay.* Screenland, *July 1942. Photo courtesy the* Media History Digital Library.

than smile and wave at the cowboy!"[27] She danced well, had her beautiful singing voice highlighted in duets with Autry, and knew how to ride since she was a girl. This intoxicating blend of sweetness and spice made her "the only female in Westerns whose box-office voltage would electrocute anything bigger than a cricket."[28] Asked about Gene, she unhesitatingly gushed, "I loved working with Gene, he was terrific! He was also a brilliant businessman . . . [i]t was a wonderful, rich experience."[29] *Down Mexico Way* plus *Sierra Sue* (1941), *Cowboy Serenade*, *Heart of the Rio Grande*, and *Home in Wyomin'* (all 1942) remain her personal cinematic legacy.

Offscreen the ebullient brunette loved jitterbug and swing, but shunned the typical social scene, choosing instead to spend her free time "chasing out to some army camp"[30] to entertain the troops. (Billy and Ella enjoyed doing the same, touring with the USO.) Fay made pictures through 1946, including the "patriotic . . . good solid hokum"[31] *Remember Pearl Harbor* (1942) with Don Barry. She also did a bit of radio, guesting on *Pabst's Blue Ribbon Town* hosted by Groucho Marx and featuring Virginia O'Brien and Leo Gorcey, episodes of Dinah Shore's 1943 program, and Don Ameche and Cass Daley's in 1944.[32]

The Gilberts decided they were ready to share their love with a child, and so in June 1941 they adopted an eleven-year-old boy, Barry. Press photos showed him sitting on Billy's knee, smiling as a beaming Ella looked on.[33] Unspeakable tragedy befell them on December 7, 1942.[34] Allegedly distraught over being scolded by his grandmother Eva, Barry Gilbert shot himself in the chest with a rifle. He left two notes, one for the general public taking full responsibility, and the other for his grandparents. "I love you with all my heart. Tell mother and dad I am grateful for all they have done for me." Ella and Billy were away on a bond-selling tour; grandfather Bob discovered the body.[35]

In 1945, Fay married actor Steve Cochran, best known for his tough-guy roles in films such as *White Heat* (1949). It was disastrous: "[t]hat was the worst decision I ever made."[36] The marriage was already over when she costarred with Bert Lahr in the 1946-1948 Broadway revival of *Burlesque*. "It was a hilarious evening . . . Fay McKenzie . . . was fetching and led the burlesque chorus with a voice that can actually sing . . . this version is really comical."[37]

She and Cochran divorced in 1947, and her second marriage a year later to screenwriter Tom Waldman was a lot happier. "[Tom was] the dearest, funniest, cutest guy . . . [i]t was the happiest time of my life."[38] (It lasted until Waldman's death in 1985.) Fay left Hollywood to raise their two children, voice actor Tom Waldman Jr.

and writer Madora McKenzie Kibbe, but kept current with classes at Lee Strasberg's Actors Studio.

Silence from the McKenzie girls until the late 1950s, when Ida Mae came roaring back in the character actor's dream: television. Through 1971, Ida Mae guested on tons of shows including *My Three Sons*, *The Donna Reed Show*, *The Andy Griffith Show*, *The Big Valley*, and *Perry Mason*. She was also a frequent supporting player on *The Red Skelton Hour*. Ida Mae's most colorful job, however, was as contestant coordinator for *The Hollywood Squares*. "She was a big woman who loved to wear bright-colored muumuus. . . ." remembered host Peter Marshall. "[S]he treated her contestants as if they were privates in the army . . . but they all loved her."[39] Two more minor roles followed, in *Soylent Green* (1973) and *Lepke* (1975), and then Ida Mae retired for good. She never married nor had children. Ida Mae died on June 27, 1986 at age 75.[40]

Ella was content to remain out of the limelight. Her beloved Billy died in 1971,[41] due to complications from an earlier stroke. She found companionship again seven months later, marrying Edward Sweeney in April of 1972.[42] The marriage lasted until her death on April 23, 1987, at age 76.[43]

Fay did some TV, but had more significant work in two modern masterpieces. She was the "woman laughing in the mirror" during the party scene in *Breakfast at Tiffany's* (1961). Director and friend Blake Edwards had actor Stanley Adams' hat set on fire to trigger her laughing fit; little did he know that the stunt was not only unnecessary, but unnoticed. ". . . [I] am terribly, terribly nearsighted. I had no idea he was trying to do anything to make me laugh."[44] Seven years later, she was Mrs. Clutterbuck in *The Party* (1968). "An unusual project even for today's experimental market,"[45] the film was almost completely devoid of dialogue but bursting with the comic genius of Peter Sellers. Credit (and birdie num-nums) went to the Edwards trifecta of scriptwriters: Edwards himself, Fay's husband Tom Waldman, and his brother Frank Waldman, the same three who also collaborated on the Pink Panther films. Fay's last credit was also for Edwards, a bit role in *S.O.B.* (1981). As of this writing, the wonderful Fay McKenzie is still with us, happily reminiscing about her career and giving laughter-filled interviews.

1   Erickson, Hal. "Bob McKenzie." *Fandango*. Web. Accessed June 22, 2015. <http://www.fandango.com/bobmckenzie/biography/p47711>

2   Magers, Boyd, and Michael Fitzgerald. "An Interview With . . . Fay McKenzie." *Western Clippings*. Web. Accessed June 19, 2015.< http://www.westernclippings.com/interview/faymckenzie_interview.shtml>

3   "At the Theatres." The *Minneapolis Journal* (MN), December 13, 1904.

4   Oshkosh *Daily Northwestern* (WI), October 18, 1904.

5   "United States Census, 1920," database with images, FamilySearch(https://family-search.org/ark:/61903/1:1:MHQF-GS2 : accessed July 27 2015), Robert B Mckenzie, Los Angeles Assembly District 63, Los Angeles, California, United States; citing sheet 4A, family 98, NARA microfilm publication T625 (Washington D.C.: National Archives and Records Administration, n.d.); FHL microfilm 1,820,106.

6   Kiehn, David. "Essanay Studio Staff Directory." *Essanay Centers, St. Augustine College*. Web. Accessed June 20, 2015. <http://essanaystudios.org/>

7   Squier, Emma-Lindsay. "Kids of the Camera." *Picture-Play*, August 1921.

8   "'So Long Buddy' Featuring Messinger Completed." *Motion Picture News*, June 9, 1923.

9   "Noel Smith Directing Buddy Messinger." *Motion Picture News*, May 26, 1923.

10  "The Record of Deaths." The New York Dramatic Mirror, February 15, 1911.

11  Marshall, Peter (2002). *Backstage With the Original Hollywood Square*. Thomas Nelson Inc.

12  "Weak Comedy Doesn't Register, Star Has Conventional Role." *Film Daily*, January 12, 1919.

13  Ferri, Roger. "State Rights Reviews: A Knight of the West." *Exhibitors Trade Review*, November 5, 1921.

14  "United States Census, 1930," database with images, FamilySearch(https://family-search.org/ark:/61903/1:1:XCFL-TKM : accessed July 27 2015), Robert B Mckenzie, Beverly Hills, Los Angeles, California, United States; citing enumeration district (ED) 0842, sheet 10A, family 293, line 18, NARA microfilm publication T626 (Washington D.C.: National Archives and Records Administration, 2002), roll 124; FHL microfilm 2,339,859.

15  Forde, Arthur. "As Seen and Heard by Arthur Forde." *Hollywood Filmograph*, July 9, 1932.

16  "Ella McKenzie." *The Three Stooges Online Filmography*. n.d. Web. Accessed June 29, 2015. <http://www.threestooges.net/cast/actor/ 248>

17  Maltin, Leonard (1973). *The Real Stars*. Curtis Books.

18  Williams, Whitney. "Hollywood Newsreel." Hollywood, January 1938.

19  Maltin, *The Real Stars*.

20  Magers and Fitzgerald, "An Interview With . . . Fay McKenzie."

21  "Robert McKenzie." *The Three Stooges Online Filmography*. n.d. Web. Accessed June 2 9, 2015. <http://www.threestooges.net/cast/actor/ 125>

22  Okuda, Ted and Edward Watz (1998). *The Columbia Comedy Shorts: Two-Reel Hollywood Film Comedies*, 1933-1958. McFarland Classics.

23  "Public Member Tree," Ancestry.com, Family tree by "allmyleaves2B", profile for Eva Belle Heazlit (b.Nov 1889 d. Sep 1967). Web. Accessed July 19, 2015.

24 Magers and Fitzgerald, "An Interview With . . . Fay McKenzie."

25 Ibid.

26 Howard, George. "Oomph On the Range." *Hollywood*, May 1942.

27 Magers and Fitzgerald, "An Interview With . . . Fay McKenzie."

28 Howard, "Oomph."

29 Magers and Fitzgerald, "An Interview With . . . Fay McKenzie."

30 Howard, "Oomph."

31 "Reviews of the New Films: 'Remember Pearl Harbor.'" *Film Daily*, May 11, 1942.

32 "Fay Mckenzie." *RUSC Old Time Radio*. n.d. Web. Accessed July 5, 2015. <http://www.rusc.com/old-time-radio/Fay- McKenzie.aspx?t=2980>

33 "Comedian's Son Takes Own Life." The *Binghamton Press* (NY), December 9, 1942.

34 Date: 1942-12-07. Ancestry.com. California, Death Index, 1940-1997 [database on-line]. Provo, UT, USA: Ancestry.com Operations Inc, 2000.

35 "Comedian's Son Suicide, Say Police." *Reading Eagle* (PA), December 8, 1942.

36 Magers and Fitzgerald, "An Interview With . . . Fay McKenzie."

37 Currie, George. "Theater: Bert Lahr Arrives in Flatbush in 'Burlesque'; Summer Is Here." *Brooklyn Eagle*, June 16, 1948.

38 Magers and Fitzgerald, "An Interview With . . . Fay McKenzie."

39 Marshall, *Backstage With the Original Hollywood Square.*

40 Date: 1986-06-29. Ancestry.com. California, Death Index, 1940-1997 [database on-line]. Provo, UT, USA: Ancestry.com Operations Inc, 2000. Original data: State of California. California Death Index, 1940-1997. Sacramento, CA, USA: State of California Department of Health Services, Center for Health Statistics.

41 "Deaths and Funerals: Gilbert Dies." *Aiken Standard* (SC), September 24, 1971.

42 Ancestry.com. California, Marriage Index, 1960-1985 [database on-line]. Provo, UT, USA: Ancestry.com Operations Inc, 2007. Original data: State of California. California Marriage Index, 1960-1985. Microfiche. Center for Health Statistics, California Department of Health Services, Sacramento, California.

43 Date: 1987-04-23. Ancestry.com. California, Death Index, 1940-1997 [database on-line]. Provo, UT, USA: Ancestry.com Operations Inc, 2000. Original data: State of California. California Death Index, 1940-1997. Sacramento, CA, USA: State of California Department of Health Services, Center for Health Statistics.

44 Wasson, Sam (2011). *Fifth Avenue, 5 A.M.: Audrey Hepburn in Breakfast at Tiffany's.* Aurum Press.

45 "'The Party' To Have World Premiere in P.S." The Desert Sun (Palm Springs, FL), March 16, 1968.

## Other Sources:

"Candidly Yours." *Modern Screen*, July 1941.

"Casts of Current Photoplays." *Photoplay*, December 1934.

"Fay McKenzie." IBDb – *The Internet Broadway Database*. Web. Accessed June 21, 2015. <http://www.ibdb.com/person.php?id=105606>

"Laughing it Off in 1928-29 with Paramount-Christie." *Exhibitors Herald and Moving Picture World*, June 16, 1928.

Linet, Beverly. "Information Desk." *Modern Screen*, February 1947.

Q, Don. "Hollywood." *Cine-Mundial*, March 1942.

"Sincere Note Puts This Film Over." *Exhibitors Herald*, December 29, 1923.

S. D., Trav. "On the REAL Snooky, and By That I Mean The Humanzee." *Travalanche*, October 23, 2013. Web. Accessed June 12, 2015. <https://travsd.wordpress. com/2013/10/23/on-the-real-snookie/>

Servo, A. Lopez. "La Joven a Quien Abraza Gene Autry." *Cine-Mundial*, August 1942.

Sid, "Film Reviews: The Last Warning." *Variety*, January 9, 1929.

"United States Census, 1940," database with images, FamilySearch(https://family-search.org/ark:/61903/1: 1:K97C-NG7 : accessed June 29 2015), Fay Mckenzie in household of Robert Mckenzie, Tract 386, West Hollywood, Beverly Hills Judicial Township, Los Angeles, California, United States; citing enumeration district (ED) 19-60, sheet 7B, family 151, NARA digital publication T 627 (Washington, D. C: National Archives and Records Administration, 2012), roll 222.

# Chapter 9:
# Beatriz and Vera Michelena

*Beatriz (L) and Vera Michelena,* Motion Picture News, *January 29, 1916. Photo courtesy the* Media History Digital Library.

Beatriz Michelena was a prima donna, and didn't care who knew it. In fact, she would have been upset if you called her anything else. She was born c.1890 in New York City (some sources say California1) to Frances Lenord, a pianist and opera singer, and Fernando Michelena, a famous Venezuelan tenor.[2] Her father was also an acclaimed vocal teacher; in *Five Years of Vocal Study under Fernando Michelena,* student Maria Antonia Field described his method as ". . . simple because it was so natural . . . [with] a marvelous patience and evenness of disposition."[3] Fernando undertook the training of Beatriz and her sister Vera, as well, both in opera and in drama. When Vera headed to New York City to make her debut, Beatriz remained under her father's tutelage in San Francisco, performing in *Princess Chic* and other local productions. She was incredibly proud of Fernando and never

*Beatriz circa her film debut.* Moving Picture World, *November 28, 1914. Photo courtesy the* Media History Digital Library.

missed a chance to praise him; sometimes too much, as *Photoplay* noted: "It is almost unbelievable about an actress, but it is a fact that it is nearly impossible to get Miss Michelena to talk about herself, for she insists on talking mostly about her 'Daddy'. She is under the impression that her 'Daddy' is the most remarkable man in the world. . . ."[4]

By 1907, however, another man entered her life: George Middleton, an automobile dealer with a prominent social profile. Beatriz and George married on March 3, their relationship the result of a rekindled childhood romance. The wedding was a quiet one, at the home of her old friend Margaret Mc-Govern, who was also her maid of honor. The groom's brother Thomas was best man, and there is mention of "relatives and a few friends"[5] in attendance, but none of the Michelenas are mentioned by name; strange, given Fernando's distinction and Vera's quickly rising fame. The happy couple honeymooned in Los Angeles for a few weeks, then settled in San Rafael, where Beatriz stayed out of the spotlight for two years.

She returned to the stage in 1910 for *The White Hen*, a musical comedy starring Max Dill. Warmly welcomed back with a "full ovation" and a "small fortune"[6] of flowers, Beatriz should have been over the moon, yet after only a few performances she wrote a scathing letter to her company manager: ". . . I am forced to give you my two weeks' notice . . . [m]y reason for doing this is because you have not lived up to your many agreements with me, particularly in relation to your publicity work. . . ."[7]

The newly-minted Michelena-Middleton objected to being billed under New York musical comedy actress Lora Lieb, one of Jesse Lasky's "Beauties" during the mogul's Vaudeville days. How could they expect her, "the daughter of one of the greatest Fausts that ever sang a high C," to sully the Michelena name with second billing? They should be grateful for her very presence, since George, aside from being "amply able to provide her with the luxuries her southern nature demanded," also "didn't think much" of musical comedy and wasn't crazy about her starring in a genre he felt beneath her talents.[8]

It's obvious that Beatriz felt supplanted by Lora Lieb. Here was some East Coast usurper getting all the cheers and raucous applause! Michelena insisted she had no resentment over Lieb's top billing, yet backhanded her by claiming the musicians called her voice "infinitely better." The San Francisco Call had a field day, making much of its native daughter's beauty, breeding, and unequaled voice. Lieb is merely "the blonde lady." There is no record of Lieb's response, if any, but Michelena's insecurity was clear. "I do not enjoy working where there is friction,"[9] said Beatriz, terminating her contract without incident. (I suspect, after all the drama, she was not greatly missed.) She instead took a limited engagement as lead in The Kissing Girl, produced by John Slocum, who discovered her and Vera as young ladies. The production paired her with good friend Texas Guinan, future queen of the speakeasies, and had songs specially inserted to show off her voice. The plum assignment lasted only four performances; George "refused consent"[10] for her to permanently join the touring company. He claimed there were reasons he and his wife couldn't travel, and after several more singing engagements, including the 1913 Mechanics' Fair (an engineering/auto show), it was time to unveil them.

Vera Michelena was six years older than her sister, and while she was incredibly popular on stage, she never quite reached the same level of motion picture notoriety as did Beatriz. Born in New York on June 16, 1885 (again, some sources say California), both she and her younger sister were sent to the Convent of San Miguel for the academic half of their education, with "Daddy" undertaking the artistic half.

John Slocum discovered Vera in 1902 singing in chapel, and a contract was drawn up that same day for a role in (you guessed it!) *Princess Chic*. She quickly impressed everyone and within six months had obtained the prima donna's position. She starred in *The Jewel of Asia*, then took the lead in two musical comedies, *The School Girl* and *The Yankee Consul*. Both gave her ample opportunity to show off her excellent vocal range and dark exotic beauty. By 1906, she was making her debut on Broadway in *The Tourist*, where her "very effectively given"

*Vera, two years after her discovery. Theatre Magazine, May 1904. Photo courtesy the Internet Archive.*

rendition of the play's love theme gained a nod from a *New York Times* reviewer.[11] She toured Boston and Philadelphia in 1907 with *The Snow Man* (later on Broadway as *The Girls from Holland*), and then it was back to the Great White Way in 1908 for *Funabashi* and *The Waltz Dream*. The press was nothing but encouraging, calling her "beautiful" and "destined to become a star."[12]

That fall, after a trip overseas to England and France, she joined the touring company for the hit Broadway musical *The Soul Kiss*, where she met her first husband, musical director Paul Schindler. From 1910 through 1911, she appeared in numerous productions both in New York and Chicago. In one of them, *The Flirting Princess*, she introduced the Vampire Dance, inspired by both the Burne-Jones painting and Kipling poem; both sources would also be the inspiration for Theda Bara's best known film, 1915's *A Fool There Was*. Vera then won the prestigious post of "principal" in the *Ziegfeld Follies of 1914*, sharing the stage with such luminaries as Leon Errol, Ann Pennington, Ed Wynn, and Bert Williams. From there her career skyrocketed: she starred in *Ned Wayburn's Town Topics* (1915) and had the lead in the hit comedy *Flo- Flo* (1917-18). She was at her peak, and it was time to invade Beatriz's territory: motion pictures.

George Middleton had initially set up the California Motion Picture Company in 1912 to make promotional films for his business, but it blossomed into a complete film studio by 1914. It was financed by a group of businessmen, including personal friend Charles Crocker, owner of the St. Francis Hotel and director of the Crocker National Bank. Their plan was "exclusively to feature adaptations from famous books, plays, and operas."[13] They wanted to be profitable enough to lure more filmmakers to San Rafael and turn it into a miniature Hollywood. The CMPC already had two stars ready to do just that: the gorgeous California scenery, and Beatriz Michelena.

Press releases laid it on thick: A July 1914 article in *Motography* calls Michelena ". . . the most beautiful woman on the American operatic stage, and an actress of extraordinary versatility . . . [t] his together with her youth and ideal size, form and animation for picture work, will establish her immediately as one of the greatest

*Beatriz as* Salomy Jane. Motography, *November 14, 1914. Photo courtesy the Media History Digital Library.*

favorites in the silent drama."[14] Beatriz herself was coy: ". . . I was planning to go on the dramatic stage before making a plunge for grand opera when I received an offer to go into moving pictures with the California Motion Picture Corporation . . . I talked it over with Daddy and he thought it would do me a heap of good. . . ."[15] Fernando Michelena himself consented to an interview and extolled the virtues of film work, ". . . for it means the development of precisely those faculties for acting that are usually ignored by opera singers—I mean histrionic faculties."[16] The CMPC's first motion picture was *Salomy Jane* (1914), adapted from Bret Harte's beloved novel of the Gold Rush. George Middleton, as producer/director, could hardly have picked a better vehicle.

*Salomy Jane* is the story of Salomy Jane Clay, the beautiful miner's daughter rescued from a thug's unwanted advances by a mystery man; later, she repays the favor when said man is wrongly captured and almost executed for a robbery he did not

*Vera and Harry Spingler in* The Devil's Playground. Exhibitors Herald, *June 1, 1918. Photo courtesy the* Media History Digital Library.

commit. Starring Beatriz Michelena in the lead, the cast also included House Peters ("The Actor with a Thousand Emotions"), Harold Entwistle (uncle of Peg, of Hollywood sign infamy), and future Western star Jack Holt. The history and lush landscape were touted as frequently as the players; publicity stunts included filling a theater lobby with a small forest of redwood tree saplings, and driving a stagecoach through the streets, "filled with typical pioneer characters."[17] The film was a smashing success, getting a terrific reception with a test audience (including actress Mabel Taliaferro), packing theaters, and garnering reviews of "masterpiece," "splendid," and "unsurpassable."[18] [19] Beatriz herself received good notices for both her acting and fearless athleticism: ". . . [s]he has to race up and down a mountain road . . . [l]eap through a tangled field . . . [Beatriz] has astounding qualities of stamina and courage."[20] The CMPC was officially on the map, and George promised Beatriz that he would make her into another Mary Pickford.

Though "Greaser" and "Latin Lover" stereotypes abounded for Latinos/Hispanics in silent films, Beatriz, like fellow silent actress Myrtle Gonzalez, avoided them primarily by playing characters of non-Latin descent. She starred in further CMPC productions: *Mrs. Wiggs of the Cabbage Patch* (1914), *Mignon, The Lily of Poverty Flat, A Phyllis of the Sierras, Salvation Nell, The Rose of the Misty Pool* (all 1915), and *The Woman Who Dared* (1916). She smiled from the cover of *Photoplay*, had a glamorous rotogravure in *Picture Play*, and attended the first annual Seattle Screen Ball (where she fainted from the crush of fans and was carried to safety by Wallace Reid). Her performance in *The Unwritten Law* (1916) was heralded as ". . . reaching her greatest height [in a] role of tremendous pathos."[21] She wrote a syndicated newspaper column, "Talks with Screen-Struck Girls", where she advised budding actresses of tomorrow that "[r]eal ability plus a lot of grit are the only things that may eventually place a girl at the summit."[22] She should have taken her own advice.

By the time Vera appeared in her first film, *Driftwood* (1916), her marriage was washed up. After a stint in the hospital for "appendicitis" (often early publicity shorthand for, well, everything but appendicitis) she filed for divorce, claiming "statuary offenses committed by the defendant in Chicago."[23] Whatever caused the death of her marriage, her mourning period was brief; she was already married to costar Harry Spingler by the time *Driftwood* was released. Reviews were generally positive, with *Motion Picture World* calling her "versatile."[24] 1917 brought them back together for *The Devil's Playground*, "a remarkable expose of the dangers of Broadway . . . the demoralization the dance halls work upon young people."[25] The film was heavily advertised as "the most pretentious photodrama of life in the gay metropolis ever produced."[26] ("Pretentious" was still largely complementary in the 1910s.) Vera was called "excellent and convincing," the rest of the cast "competent and well-balanced."[27]

Even though the camera liked her, and she certainly flourished before it, these were the only two films Michelena ever made. By 1919 she was back onstage, reprising her Vampire Dance in *Take it from Me* with musical comedy actor and Julliard-educated composer Fred Hillebrand (remember him, he's important later), then off to Boston for *Betty Be Good*. Her last appearances in the legitimate theater were in the *Ziegfeld Follies of 1921* (again a principal), and *Love Dreams* (1921).

Beatriz's increasingly large ego, oblivious to mediocre box office returns, led to a contract dispute and subsequent break with the CMPC in 1917. She and George Middleton promptly formed their own production company, Beatriz Michelena Pictures, where she appeared in *Just Squaw* (1919), *Heart of Juanita* (1919), and *The Flame of Hellgate* (1920). These three films, along with *The Price Woman Pays* (1919), are still listed as being from the CMPC, but she may have obtained the rights to them in the split. Interestingly, *The Price Woman Pays* includes footage from *Faust* (1917), never completed due to the contract dispute. With that one exception, all the BMP films are Westerns, again casting the beauty of northern California as her costar. None of the films were profitable; *Hellgate* was her last. Children playing with firecrackers burned down the building housing all of Michelena's films in 1931, but in 1996 the sole surviving print of *Salomy Jane* was found in Australia. It has since been restored and released on DVD. President G.W. Bush acknowledged her contribution to film in 2002 with a proclamation during National Hispanic Heritage Month.

After 1920, details of Beatriz's life become sketchy. By 1921, the California Motion Picture Corporation, as well as Beatriz Michelena Pictures, had gone bust, and George Middleton reverted to automobiles. Beatriz returned to her operatic roots, touring with the company which introduced both *Carmen* and *Madame Butterfly* to Latin America in 1927.[28] According to Geoffrey Bell's *The Golden Gate and the Silver Screen*, Beatriz and George divorced (the 1930 census shows them as still married, but it also shows Fernando's birthplace as Switzerland,[29] so take from that what you will) and she initially retired to Spain. She returned to San Rafael sometime between 1937 and 1940; real estate records from that time show the sale of most of her former studio lot. She battled rectal cancer for two years, and died of complications from a surgical procedure on October 10, 1942. She was 52.

Vera's own love dreams were momentarily shattered with a second divorce, this time on grounds of desertion, but six months later she walked down the aisle for a third time with Fred Hillebrand.

*A playful Beatriz.* Photoplay, *February 1915. Photo courtesy the* Media History Digital Library.

(Told you he was important.) It was a successful and lucrative professional match: they starred together in various popular Vaudeville revues through the 1920s. *Variety* chastised Hillebrand for one appearance, where he "confused vulgarity with humor." The comments he made about his wife's appearance in tights had the "house . . . guessing how Hillebrand was going to work a week in Boston with his act and get away with it."[30] Boston was one of the strictest regions; it was common for acts to have a clean-cut "Boston version" to prevent being shut down. (Too bad history did not record what Hillebrand said!)

The two made a successful match off-stage, as well. They were still happily married in 1940, Vera retired and Fred working in films and television until 1953, and as a songwriter with membership in ASCAP.[31] Vera Michelena passed away, aged 77, at her Queens home on August 28, 1961.

1  1920; Census Place: San Rafael, Marin, California; Roll: T625_120; Page: 13B; Enumeration District: 94; Image: 939. Ancestry.com. 1920 United States Federal Census [database on-line]. Provo, UT, USA: Ancestry.com Operations Inc., 2010. Accessed Oct 17, 2014.

2  California, San Francisco Area Funeral Home Records, October 1942, Beatriz Michelena Middleton, parents, Fernando Michelena, Frances Lenord. Ancestry.com. Accessed Oct 17, 2014.

3  Field, Maria Antonia (1922). *Five Years of Vocal Study Under Fernando Michelena.*, C.D.L.

4  "The Girl on the Cover." Photoplay, February 1915.

5  "Marriage Comes as Sequel to Romance of School Days: George E. Middleton Weds Miss Michelena." The San Francisco Call, March 4, 1907.

6  "Noted Trio Has Powerful Play." The *San Francisco Call*. October 27, 1910.

7  "Actress Quits After Quarrel Over Publicity: Beatriz Middleton Balks at Playing 'Second Fiddle' to Lora Lieb". The *San Francisco Call*. December 1, 1910.

8  Ibid.

9  Ibid.

10  "Singer Migrates Back to Opera: Beatriz Michelena-Middleton to Appear for Three Nights in 'The Kissing Girl.'" The *San Francisco Call,* December 6, 1910.

11  "A Mystic Maze of Girls, Song, Color." *New York Times*, August 26, 1906.

12  "Young Singer Climbs Fame's Ladder Fast." The *San Francisco Call*, January 19, 1906.

13  "California Motion Picture Corporation." *Motography*, July 4, 1914.

14  Ibid.

15  "The Girl on the Cover." *Photoplay*, February 1915.

16  "The Movies as a Training School." *Motography*, August 22, 1914.

17  "Attractive Publicity." *Motography*, November 14, 1914.

18  Condon, Charles R. "'Salomy Jane' a Masterpiece." *Motography*, November 14, 1914.

19  Harrison, Louis Reeves. "Salomy Jane." *Moving Picture World*, October 1914.

20  "Earns Her Salary." *Motography*, November 21, 1914.

21  "'Unwritten Law' Best Medium for Star's Talents." *Motion Picture News*, January 15, 1916.

22  Michelena, Beatriz. "Talks with Screen-Struck Girls." *Prescott Journal-Miner* (AZ), February 6, 1916.

23  "Vera Michelena Wins Divorce." New York Clipper, May 30, 1917.

24  "Vera Michelena, 'Driftwood' Star, is Versatile Actress." *Motion Picture News*, January 29, 1916.

25  "Film Shows Up Broadway." *New York Clipper*, May 16, 1917.

26  Advertisement in *Moving Picture World*, May 11, 1918, p.813.

27  Sewell, C.S. "The Devil's Playground." *Moving Picture World*, January 26, 1918.

28  Fregoso, Rosa Linda (2003). *meXicana Encounters: The Making of Social Identities on the Borderlands*. University of California Press.

29  1930; Census Place: San Rafael, Marin, California; Roll: 176; Page: 10A; Enumeration District: 0020. Ancestry.com. 1930 United States Federal Census [database on-line]. Provo, UT, USA: Ancestry.com Operations, Inc., 2012. Accessed Oct 17, 2014.

30  "Keith's Boston." *Variety*, February 21, 1924.

31  1940; Census Place: New York, Queens, New York; Roll: T627_2736; Page: 3B; Enumeration District: 41-818. Ancestry.com. 1940 United States Federal Census [database on-line]. Provo, UT, USA: Ancestry.com Operations, Inc., 2012. Accessed Oct 17, 2014.

## Other Sources:

Bell, Geoffrey (1984). *The Golden Gate and the Silver Screen*. Associated University Press.

Brightwell, Eric. "?Silencio! – The Hispanic & Latino experience in the silent era." *Amoeblog*, September 19, 2009. Web. Accessed Oct 20, 2014. <http://www.amoeba.com/blog/2009/09/eric-s-blog/-silencio-the-hispanic-latino-experience-in-the-silent-era.html>

Bush, George W. (September 14, 2002). "National Hispanic Heritage Month, 2002." *The White House*. Web. Accessed Nov 1, 2014. <http://georgewbush-whitehouse.archives.gov/news/releases/2002/09/20020914-3.html>

Finley, J. (February 17, 1955). "Litchfield v. County of Marin, 130 Cal.App.2d 806". *Lawlink: the attorney network*. Web. Accessed Nov 1, 2014. <http://www.lawlink.com/research/CaseLevel3/29741>

Flom, Eric L (2009). *Silent Film Stars on the Stages of Seattle: A History of Performances by Hollywood Notables*. McFarland Press.

Gladysz, Thomas. "Once Lost Film Returns to Bay Area". *The Huffington Post*, September 19, 2012. Web. Accessed Nov 1, 2014. <http://www.huffingtonpost.com/thomas-gladysz/salomy-jane-film_b_1893879.html>

Lyons, MaryAnne. "Beatriz Michelena." In Jane Gaines, Radha Vatsal, and Monica Dall'Asta, eds. *Women Film Pioneers Project*. Center for Digital Research and Scholarship. New York, NY: Columbia University Libraries, 2013. Web. Accessed Oct 30, 2014. <https://wfpp.cdrs.columbia.edu/pioneer/ccp-beatriz-michelena/>

# Chapter 10:
# Mary and Florence Nash

*Mary Nash, Motion Picture News, July 10, 1915, and Florence Nash, Motion Picture News, December 19, 1914. Photos courtesy the Media History Digital Library.*

A lot of things were born in Troy, a city along the eastern edge of the Hudson River in New York: Arrow Collars; "A Visit from St. Nicholas;" Sanforization (a method of pre-shrinking fabric so the finished garment retains its size when washed); and two little girls named Mary and Florence Ryan. Mary was born first, on August 15, 1884;[1] Florence came two years later, on October 2, 1886.[2] (Both ladies habitually tweaked their birth years, and it's not unusual to find a discrepancy of five years or more.)

Shortly after the sudden death of their father, corporate lawyer James H. Ryan, in January 1894,[3][4] their mother, Ellen, married theatrical manager Philip Nash, "one of the most popular of the early Keith managers"[5] and Vaudeville bookers for the United

Booking Office. They moved to Manhattan, where the girls took his last name[6] and called him Pop until he, too, died suddenly in October 1914.[7]

Nash left Ellen and the girls well provided for. Private school for Mary and Florence, at the Convent of St. Anne in Montreal, and the American Academy of Dramatic Arts for Mary (whether Florence attended is undetermined).[8] Mary hit the boards first, taking over for the elfin Marie Doro in *The Girl From Kay's* (1904). Celebrated producer Charles Frohman was instantly smitten by her "attractive personality and undoubted talents"[9] and added her to *Alice-Sit-By-The- Fire* (1905), starring Ethel Barrymore. That's right: Mary made her Christmas Day New York debut supporting The First Lady of the American Theater. Two more ingénue parts opposite Barrymore followed, in *Captain Jinks of the Horse Marines* and *The Silver Box* (both 1907). The roles were good, but Frohman sensed something in her beyond "impersonating sweet and innocent young things."[10] She stretched out into leads and soon was knee-deep in back-to- back hits: 1909's *The City*, with which she toured into 1911; and *The Woman*, which also went on the road until 1913.

How Florence got her start is a matter of debate. Did she ditch school one day to perform with comedian John Bunny's stock company?[11] Did her parents try reverse psychology, sending the stage-struck Flo to sweat through six weeks at the Bijou Theatre in Philadelphia, only to have her jubilance backfire their plan?[12] The only certainty is that she was definitely doing stock in 1906. Her New York debut one year later as the "lisping girl" in *The Boys of Company B* (1907) stormed Broadway and led to another lisping role in *Miss Hook of Holland* (1907-08). When she was asked again to lisp for an upcoming role in *Algeria* (1908), she "set her foot down solidly" [13] and played it straight, to continued acclaim.

Florence spent 1908-1909 in DeWolf Hopper's touring company of *The Pied Piper*, then returned to standard ingénue parts. She officially hit her stride with the one-act Vaudeville play *In 1999* (1912). Written by William deMille, the spoof imagined a world where ladies worked at the office and gentlemen cooked, cleaned, and cared for the children at home. The sketch relied on gender-swapped tropes for laughs: husband Rollo (Joseph W. Jefferson) in tears because wife Jean (Nash) spent too much time at the club; Jean puffing a cigarette, swearing about how independently-minded men have gotten; and a love triangle where the "weaker" Rollo is led astray by the assertive Florence (Minnette Barrett). DeMille's not so subtle dig at the suffragette movement tickled audiences tremendously. Florence, as Jean, "strut[ted] and bellow[ed] like the mere masculine creature that woman is presumably to become by 1999." [14] It was a bit of a one-trick pony, and some felt the script lacked punch, but what it had was novel, zesty, and marvelously fun. Even Mary, who refused offers for years, was inspired by the runaway success to play Vaudeville herself two years later in *The Watch Dog* (1914). [15]

In September 1912, Florence left the show to join *Within the Law* at Broadway's Eltinge Theater. The hard-boiled, slang-spewing con artist Aggie Lynch was arguably the play's best role, and she didn't disappoint; "her success on the opening night was sweeping." [16] The crime drama enjoyed 541 performances—many of them packed to capacity—and a lucrative cross-country tour. *Within the Law* spawned numerous revivals and five film versions, including *Paid* (1930) with Joan Crawford.

Notoriety, charisma, critical admiration . . . both ladies had it in spades. "To Florence Nash . . . too great credit cannot be given for the excellence of her work." [17] As for Mary, "the applause she elicits in constantly growing measure is . . . a real tribute to the feelings of the audience." [18] The sisters were flattered but modest. "The great artist should be able to sink his personality in a character part," pronounced a humble Mary. Both felt "[t]he actor's value is in his interpretation of the playwright's character." [19] Whether the play or the players got them noticed, noticed they were, and not just by the matinee crowd. Motion pictures came calling, and Mary and Florence confidently answered.

This time, little sister grabbed the brass ring first, signing for the lead in *Springtime* (1914), the Life-Photo Film Corporation's version of the Booth Tarkington period piece. Florence played Madeline, a role written for Mabel Taliaferro in the original 1909 stage version. Part of the picture was filmed on location in New

*Florence in Springtime.* Motion Picture News, *December 5, 1914.* Photo courtesy the Media History Digital Library.

Orleans' French Quarter, lending poignant realism to the War of 1812 romance. By all accounts Florence made the jump from stage to screen beautifully, "handl[ing] the part with the skill which one would expect . . . to equal advantage in the easiest scenes and in the difficult ones."[20] *Springtime* as a whole gained good notices, "an unusually attractive story . . . obtaining the impression of the period to a remarkable degree."[21] Mary also joined Life-Photo, her showcase being *The Unbroken Road* (1915). The political drama got points for attractive cinematography but underachieved in the plot department, "not as full of punch and originality as it might be."[22] The sincere but weak cast was largely to blame: "had they asserted themselves more . . . the picture would have been much more convincing."[23] Mary at least was "a fortunate choice"[24] as the heroine, Constance Turner.

Both sisters left Life-Photo directly afterwards, and went in opposite directions. Florence returned to the stage in *Sinners* (1915) at New York's Playhouse Theater, while Mary signed a new contract with Knickerbocker Star Features. Knickerbocker, "gratified

*Mary Nash, Alexander Gaden, and William H. Tooker in* The Unbroken Road. Motography, *May 29, 1915. Photo courtesy the* Media History Digital Library.

in having secured the services of Miss Nash,"[25] assigned her the artistic drama *The Tides of Time* (1915). She was heavily promoted, name above the title in ads proclaiming her "one of the best known modern young actresses of the legitimate stage."[26] The film, inspired by an odd blend of Shakespeare and Poe, required Mary to play the same woman from ages twenty to eighty. The result had somewhat of a weird aspect, although its intensity remains."[27]

The stage beckoned and Mary closed out the year in three different Broadway productions, but 1916 saw her back on the screen in *Arms and the Woman*, a WWI drama that provided Edward G. Robinson's screen debut. It was Mary's last film for a while: before the ink on her new contract with World was dry, she was touring with the smash hit, *The Man Who Came Back*, fresh off its 1916-17 triumph on Broadway with her in the featured spot. After a year of not working—mostly because she no longer wanted gimmicky, "slangy" roles—Florence moved audiences in *The Land of the Free* (1917) at the Forty Eighth Street Theater. She played Russian immigrant and sweatshop worker Sonya Marinoff "so humanly that one loses sight of the footlights."[28] It only lasted 32 performances but "won Florence Nash's point for her."[29]

1918 brought both women excitement of another sort. Florence published a book of poetry, *June Dusk: and Other Poems*, dedicated to Mary and her mother "for whom my love is too big to put into a poem."[30] Popular opinion glowingly rated her "as great a poet as she [was] an actress."[31] (This author agrees; some of her verse is actually quite good.)  She was slated for the lead in *The Melting of Molly*, a musical comedy of the sort she did before *Within the Law*, but the role went instead to *Passing Show* alum Isabelle Love. Undaunted, Florence was the eponymous title character in *Remnant* (1918-19), which played 63 performances.

Mary's big event wasn't on the boards but down the aisle. She wed actor José Ruben on October 19, 1918.[32] Ruben was in several movies including an early Hitchcock, *The Man from Home* (1922), but was noteworthy for appearing in over forty-five Broadway shows over the course of his career. He and Mary were in at least three together, the first being mere days before their wedding. *I.O.U.* (1918) was an anomaly: a stage dramatization based on a film, in this case *The Cheat* (1915) with Sessue Hayakawa and Fannie Ward. The experiment was a dud; the adaptation "most unconvincing" and the change from Japanese to East Indian—at the request, it was said, by the government—"immeasurably weakened the story."[33] The marriage also fizzled quickly, and Mary was back living with her mother and sister by 1920.[34]

The 1920s were a blur of activity for the thespian sisters. Offers from Vaudeville and Broadway overflowed. Occasionally, they worked together, like the 1926 revival of *The Two Orphans* (filmed in 1921 as *Orphans of the Storm* with Lillian and Dorothy Gish), or the "emphatically melodramatic"[35] 1927 play, *Fate's Messenger*, with Mary as a drug addict and Florence as a "slangy"[36] narc. Various clubs invited Florence to lecture on theater at their soirees. "Don't ever recommend a play that's dull, just because its moral," she warned. "No play is a good play unless it is well-written and well-acted." Effort went both ways, too: "[b]ecome a great audience and you'll get fine plays. The actors . . . need your help."[37]

Neither she nor Mary needed help gathering projects, and so their names remained absent from the motion picture rosters for a time; but, by 1934, Mary's last Broadway play was two years behind

*Mary and Cary Grant in* The Philadelphia Story. Photoplay, *October 1940.*
*Photo courtesy the* Media History Digital Library.

her and she was ready to try her hand at movies again. That in-
augural year cast her with Edward Everett Hoffman in *Uncertain
Lady* (1934), followed by *College Scandal* in 1935, the same year
Florence joined her in California. Florence landed a small part in
*It's A Great Life* (1935), with William Frawley, Charles "Chic" Sale,
Joe Morrison, and Paul Kelly. The screenplay by actor Arthur
Lake revolved round the Civilian Conservation Corps, a govern-
ment project of the Depression. It also was rather dull.

Mary fared better as Eddy Arnold's wife in *Come and Get It*
(1936), then a string of juicy roles for which she is best remembered: Eddy Arnold's dotty, dollar-hemorrhaging wife *in Easy
Living* (1937); Shirley Temple's nightmare, Fräulein Rottenmeier,
in *Heidi* (1938); and malevolent Miss Minchin, the headmistress
again making Temple's life miserable in *The Little Princess* (1939).
She also worked with Joan Blondell (*The King and the Chorus
Girl*, 1937) Joel McCrea (*Wells Fargo*, 1939), and Tyrone Power
and Myrna Loy (*The Rains Came*, also 1939). Mary's lucky streak
lasted well into the 1940s, beginning with Margaret Lord, Katharine Hepburn's "frazzled – and sometimes puzzled"[38] mother in
the brilliantly screwy *The Philadelphia Story* (1940). Other films
included *The Human Comedy* (1943) with Mickey Rooney, the cult
favorite *Cobra Woman* (1944) with the ravishing Maria Montez,

*Those wonderful* Women, *from L to R: Florence, Phyllis Povah, Rosalind Russell, Joan Crawford, Norma Shearer, Paulette Goddard, Mary Boland, and Joan Fontaine.* Cine-Mundial, *October 1939. Photo courtesy the* Media History Digital Library.

and the musical *Yolanda and the Thief* (1945), "dripping with Technicolor"[39] and starring Fred Astaire. A year later she capped her cinematic career with *Swell Guy* (1946). Her life after retirement was quiet; she never remarried or had children. Mary Nash died at the Brentwood, California home she once shared with Florence on December 3, 1976.[40] She was 92.

Florence made her last Broadway appearance in 1930. She appeared in only one other film, but she made it count: the catty, caustically funny *The Women* (1939). Florence never married or had children. During the 1940s, she fell ill with a heart ailment which led to her death on April 2, 1950.[41] She was 64.

> "When I am dead, sing me no requiems,
> Chant me no dirges, nor weep for me tears;
> I shall pass over the flesh-chilling border
> Soul singing joyously, empty of fears."
> –Florence Nash, "When I Am Dead"

1   1 Date: 1976-12-03. Ancestry.com. California, Death Index, 1940-1997 [database on-line]. Provo, UT, USA: Ancestry.com Operations Inc, 2000. State of California. California Death Index, 1940-1997. Sacramento, CA, USA: State of California Department of Health Services, Center for Health Statistics.

2   Date: 1950-04-02. Ancestry.com. California, Death Index, 1940-1997 [database on-line]. Provo, UT, USA: Ancestry.com Operations Inc, 2000. State of California. California Death Index, 1940-1997. Sacramento, CA, USA: State of California Department of Health Services, Center for Health Statistics.

3   "Find A Grave Index," database, FamilySearch (https://familysearch.org/ark:/61903/1:1:QVLK-M3YN : accessed 28 October 2015), James H. Ryan, 1894; Burial, Troy, Rensselaer, New York, United States of America, SaintMary's Cemetery; citing record ID 97382443, Find a Grave, http://www.findagrave.com.

4   "Ryan." The Troy Irish Genealogical Society. Web. Accessed July 23, 2015. <http://rootsweb.ancestry.com/~nytigs/index.htm>

5   "Gossip of Plays and Players." The Brooklyn Daily Eagle, March 19, 1922.

6   Year: 1910; Census Place: Manhattan Ward 22, New York, New York; Roll: T624_1045; Page: 7A; Enumeration District: 1282; FHL microfilm: 1375058. Ancestry.com. 1910 United States Federal Census [database on-line]. Provo, UT, USA: Ancestry.com Operations Inc, 2006.

7   "Obituary: Philip Nash." New York Times, October 5, 1914.

8   Parker, John, ed. (1922). Who's Who in the Theatre, 4th ed. Small, Maynard and Co.

9   "Mary Nash." Brooklyn Life, July 11, 1903.

10   "Concerning Plays and Players: Mary Nash." The Brooklyn Daily Eagle, February 16, 1919.

11   "Who's Who on the Stage." New York Times, October 7, 1917.

12   "Gossip of Plays and Players," The Brooklyn Daily Eagle.

13   "Who's Who on the Stage," New York Times.

14   "Mock Problem Play is Rich In Satire." New York Times, February 6, 1912.

15   "In Vaudeville." New York Times, April 12, 1914.

16   "Two Clever Sisters." The New York Dramatic Mirror, February 5, 1913.

17   "Plays and Players: In Manhattan." Brooklyn Life, October 13, 1917.

18   Brooklyn Life, December 22, 1923.

19   Randolph, Ann. "Personality on the Stage." National Magazine, April 1913.

20   Pangburn, Clifford H. "Springtime." Motion Picture News, January 2, 1915.

21   Ibid.

22   Condon, Charles R. "Life Photo's 'The Unbroken Road.'" Motography, May 29, 1915.

23   Ibid.

24   Pangburn, Clifford H. "The Unbroken Road." Motion Picture News, May 29, 1915.

25   "Mary Nash Joins Knickerbocker." Motion Picture News, July 10, 1915.

26   Advertisement in Motion Picture News, July 31, 1915, pg. 105.

27   Milne, Peter. "Tides of Time." Motion Picture News, August 7, 1915.

28   "Plays and Players," Brooklyn Life.

29   "Who's Who on the Stage," New York Times.

30  Nash, Florence (1918). *June Dusk: and Other Poems*. George H. Doran Company.

31  "Eva Le Gallienne for Low-Priced Show." *New York Times*, March 10, 1928.

32  "Mary Nash and José Ruben Marry." *New York Times*, October 24, 1918.

33  photo caption in *Photoplay*, January 1919, pg. 64.

34  "United States Census, 1920," database with images, FamilySearch (https://family-search.org/ark:/61903/1:1:MJYG-2N9 : accessed 28 October 2015), Florence Nash in household of Ellen Nash, Manhattan Assembly District 7, New York, New York, United States; citing sheet 1A, family 8, NARA microfilm publication T625 (Washington D.C.: National Archives and Records Administration, n.d.); FHL microfilm 1,821,198.

35  "Nash Sisters at Palace." *New York Times*, January 4, 1927.

36  Ibid.

37  "Florence Nash Warns Against Dull Plays." *New York Times*, October 30, 1928.

38  Ashe, Brandie. "Who's that girl?: Mary Nash." *True Classics*. Wordpress. August 24, 2011. Web. Accessed August 31, 2015. <http://trueclassics.net/2011/08/24/whos-that-girl-mary-nash/>

39  "Reviews of New Films: 'Yolanda and the Thief.'" *Film Daily*, October 19, 1945.

40  "Mary Nash Dead; Character Actress Of Stage and Film." *New York Times*, December 8, 1976.

41  "Florence Nash, 60, Stage Comedienne." *New York Times*, April 3, 1950.

## Other Sources:

"Florence Nash." IBDb – *The Internet Broadway Database*. Web. Accessed August 17, 2015. <http://www.ibdb.com/Person/View/54271>

"José Ruben." IBDb – *The Internet Broadway Database*. Web. Accessed August 17, 2015. <http://www.ibdb.com/Person/View/6937>

Mary and Florence Nash papers, 1893-1974. Collection overview. *The New York Public Library Archives and Manuscripts*. Web. Accessed September 3, 2015. <http://archives.nypl.org/the/18988>

"Mary Nash." IBDb – *The Internet Broadway Database*. Web. Accessed August 17, 2015. <http://www.ibdb.com/Person/View/54277>

"Villain Is Hissed At The Orpheum." The *Brooklyn Daily Eagle*, May 14, 1912.

# Chapter 11:
# Sally O'Neil and Molly O'Day

*Sally O'Neil (L) and Molly O'Day,* Photoplay, *July 1927. Photo courtesy the* Media History Digital Library.

Not so long ago, in the not so faraway land of New Jersey, Judge Thomas Noonan Jr., a "great- hearted, upright, able and courageous man,"[1] held court with his bride, Hannah Peterson Kelly. Hannah retired from her opera career after their marriage in 1890,[2] devoting herself wholeheartedly to motherhood. By the 1910 census[3] they had an impressive roster: Thomas III, Mary, Gerard (Gerald), George, Vincent, John, Isabel, Edmund, and the two littlest, Virginia, born October 23, 1908,[4] and Suzanne, born October 16, 1909.[5] Judge Noonan was greatly respected; achieving membership in the N.J. Assembly by age 27, he deftly rose through the ranks of the New Jersey judicial system, serving as District Court Judge and City Counsel of Bayonne, as well as Counsel of Hudson County. Thanks to his eminent status, the family was financially comfortable, even able to employ some much needed servants to tend to their bustling brood.

After Judge Noonan's sudden death, the large family was thrown into chaos. Hannah eventually sold their home and moved them all to California. Little is known of the family during these years; we know the older boys served in WWI, and that Mary was a nurse with the Red Cross.[6] After the war, George was on an Olympic hockey team, and both he and Gerard ("Jerry") played pro football.[7] Virginia was away at private convent-run schools in both Staten Island and Canada, but by 1925, was back in California, dancing under the perfect Vaudeville name: Chotsie Noonan.

It was during a performance at the Ambassador Hotel that Marshall "Mickey" Neilan and his wife, actress Blanche Sweet, discovered her. He was having terrible luck finding someone as childlike and charming as Mary Pickford for his dramedy, *Mike*, when the cute and curly-haired answer appeared, quite literally, in front of him. He wasted no time asking "Chotsie" to the studio. "Golly, I was dumb," she told columnist Margaret Reid. "I didn't know who Marshall Neilan was . . . I recognized Blanche Sweet . . .[and] thought well, if here isn't old Pie-Face me getting a chance to see the inside of a studio."[8] They surreptitiously gave the seventeen-year-old a screen test, and she was exactly what they wanted: adorably spunky yet completely unaware of it, still possessing "the sweetness of childhood." She was Mike. When Neilan said she had the part, her "knees got so shaky . . . [she] was so excited and petrified and thrilled."[9]

Written and directed by Neilan and released in early 1926, *Mike* costarred Charles Murray as the father she "cures" of drinking and William Haines as the sweetheart who helps her foil train bandits. Ford Sterling, Frankie Darro, Junior Coghlan, and Muriel Frances Dana were able supporters. "Real entertainment for the masses!" cried the press. "[A] picture that rocks the fans with laugh explosions . . . and sends them home more than satisfied."[10] Chotsie, now Sally O'Neil, was off to a slam-bang start.

Suzanne followed in big sister's footsteps. "I was fourteen, lived in California, so tried for acting in the movies."[11] Older sister Isa-

*At the table, from L to R: Constance Bennett, Joan Crawford, and Sally in* Sally, Irene and Mary. Motion Picture News, *December 19, 1925. Photo courtesy the* Media History Digital Library.

bel also tried, but declared it not for her and left soon after. Suzanne's first work was as "Sue O'Neil" in Hal Roach two-reelers, including unbilled extra work in *Our Gang* shorts, and she might have floundered there if fate hadn't intervened in the form of Dorothy Mackaill. More on that later.

Filmed before *Mike* but not released until late 1925, *Sally, Irene and Mary* (1925) made superstars out of its entire cast. The film version of the popular Broadway musical featured O'Neil, Constance Bennett, and Joan Crawford as three chorus girls dealing with the consequences of being "fluttering moths around the candle of risky pleasures."[12] Some critics felt the "trite," "appallingly obvious"[13] script manipulative and false, but the cast, including William Haines as Mary's love interest, generally received good notices. O'Neil in particular earned kudos for her "bewitching personality" and "instinct for comedy."[14] She nurtured that instinct in *Battling Butler* (1926), one of the least Keatonesque of Buster Keaton's features. Loosely adapted from the hit play, Keaton is a pampered millionaire who impersonates the famous pugilist, "Battling" Butler, to impress a girl (O'Neil). When the true Butler finds out, the playboy must strap on the boxing gloves for

*Richard Barthelmess and Molly in* The Patent Leather Kid. Photoplay, *September 1927. Photo courtesy the* Media History Digital Library.

real. While not the strongest of Keaton's pictures, the chord it struck with audiences made it his most financially successful.

If you had been thumbing through *Photoplay* for the latest brickbats and bouquets, you'd probably come across promo shots of Dorothy Mackaill for *The Patent Leather Kid* (1927). Mackaill and Richard Barthelmess had done well together in *The Fighting Blade* (1923), and First National was eager for a repeat. Mackaill was, too; in fact, she was so ready to make this picture that she refused to film a previously contracted one with Jack Mulhall, *See You in Jail* (1927). First National retaliated by axing her from the payroll and recasting all her projects: the Mulhall film went to Alice Day, and "Sue O'Neill [sic], sister of Sally O'Neill, has been chosen for the Barthelmess picture."[15] (Her stage name was changed to Kitty Kelly, but after an indignant letter from an actress who had that name since birth, they went with Molly O'Day instead.) Barthelmess was the title character, brave in the ring but terrified on the battlefield, in this "powerful drama of the war."[16] He overcomes his fear and gallantly fights his way to a shocking,

*Sally, Isabel, and Molly.* Picture Play, *August 1927. Photo courtesy the* Media History Digital Library.

"smashing" climax. As popular as *The Big Parade* (1925), it restarted Barthelmess' career and earned him a Best Actor nomination at the first Academy Awards in 1929. As for Molly, "[h]er acting in this tale rivals that of Mr. Barthelmess. She is sincere and earnest . . . [and] most competent in a part that demands a great deal."[17]

The world was in love with the two Irish beauties. O'Neil was touted as MGM's Clara Bow, "a small roughneck who flaps with every excitable breath."[18] She was one of the 1926 WAMPAS Baby Stars, an honor prestigious enough to assuage her stage fright ("I'd get in front of the camera and see all those people standing around . . . I'd go perfectly stiff"[19]). Molly received the same accolade two years later, as well as one of the first stars on the Hollywood Walk of Fame, but her PR people presented her as a kind of anti-Sally, "sweet and unflapperish . . . [with] a quiet, impersonal manner."[20]

O'Neil got a welcome respite from the tasteless "ethnic" films exploiting her Irish heritage with *The Lovelorn* (1927), the first time she and Molly worked together. Georgie (O'Neil) is in love with her sister (O'Day)'s boyfriend, and turns to advice columnist Beatrice Fairfax for help on her next move. ("Beatrice Fairfax" was the pen name of the real-life syndicated columnist of "Advice to the Lovelorn," begun in 1898.) The problem is solved when the boyfriend turns out a gold-digger, and both sisters kick him to the curb. Reports circulated that O'Neil chewed out O'Day on set for a "display of temperament,"[21] but O'Day remembered it differently: "[m]

y sister was my favorite [actress] to work with."[22] Isabel and Jack also allegedly appeared in the "laughable comedy,"[23] though unaccredited (and currently unverified).

Another bit of temperament connected Molly and Dolores del Rio. A staged fight between the directors of O'Day's film *The Shepherd of the Hills* (1928) and del Rio's film *Ramona* (1928) over location rights went sour when Molly threw a "peace dinner" for everyone on both films except del Rio. Press claimed O'Day somehow missed the memo that it was all a publicity stunt and felt del Rio was responsible for the whole mess. "Are Dolores del Rio and Molly O'Day going to be lifelong enemies?"[24] Dolores allegedly blew the whole thing off, despite her husband's demands for a public apology, and the fracas passed into oblivion. There appeared to be nothing but sunny skies ahead.

Cue clouds.

"[Y]ou know I guess about my brother Jackie . . . I did everything I could for the poor kid,"[25] lamented Sally. John Noonan - "Jack" - was previously busted for assault and violation of the Volstead Act, and certainly was no stranger to trouble, but this was different. The former Marine Corps junior lightweight champion and technical director on *The Patent Leather Kid* was arrested for burglarizing the home of bandleader Ted Lewis (and Lewis wasn't happy). Noonan's alleged haul of costumes, furs, and jewelry was valued as anywhere from $10,000 to $75,000. A panicked O'Neil emptied her bank account, attempting to save him from a seven-year-stretch in Folsom Prison, and succeeded in getting him a sanity hearing, which led to a reduction of charges: one year in prison and five on probation. She didn't count on Jackie undoing her efforts by escaping from his prison work camp. He was recaptured in New York and taken to City Prison (the "Tombs"). "The trial took my last cent," Sally mused, "but I couldn't save him from prison." Her work suffered, and "the nerve-strain showed in her performance."[26] It didn't help matters that *The Battle of the Sexes* (1928), D. W. Griffith's lone foray into urbane sex comedy, received some of the worst reviews of his career. Tense and distracted, O'Neil also failed to notice her sister's very public nightmare.

*The Noonans, all in a row. Sally is first on the right, with Molly next to her.*
Photoplay, *January 1928. Photo courtesy the* Media History Digital Library.

Shortly after Molly's second picture with Barthelmess, *The Little Shepherd of Kingdom Come* (1928), First National put her on notice for being twenty pounds over her contract's weight clause. Stills from the time show a lovely young lady with chubby cheeks and sparkling eyes, an average seventeen-year-old. Average anywhere but Hollywood, where curves were out, Art Deco was in, and it was open season on fat-shaming. They said she overindulged on sweets. They said she sneaked food in private while following the dietician's rules in public.

Worst of all, the costarring role in *The Barker* (1928) was snatched out of her hands by producer Al Rockett, who chastised: "Molly, you can get as fat as you please . . . as far as we are concerned, you are through—that is, until you get down to the right physical size for our pictures."[27] In a stinging bit of turnaround, the part went to none other than Dorothy Mackaill. It was a desperate O'Day who, a month before her eighteenth birthday, went to a facility in Hot Springs Arkansas, where she had a "dietician [and] physical instructor . . . hot baths every morning and evening . . . and three times a day, spinach and lamb chops and pineapple."[28]

It also appeared she succumbed to more drastic measures, undergoing a crude liposuction-like procedure "to remove several pounds of flesh from her hips and legs."[29] Long incisions were made on her stomach, hips, and legs, and "electric needles [used] to melt the fat away."[30] A horrified George Raft, who had dated

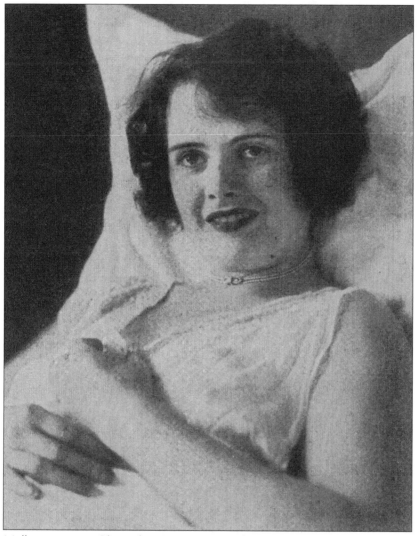

*Molly in recovery.* Photoplay, *January 1929. Photo courtesy the* Media History Digital Library.

Molly, recalled "they tried to cut the fat off . . . [w]hen they sewed her up she had seam scars running up the sides of her formerly beautiful body . . . [it] damn near killed her."[31] O'Day confessed "it seemed the only way for me to reduce . . .a great deal of nervousness follows an operation like that."[32] Recovery was slow. A glassy-eyed Molly forced a smile for *Photoplay* photogs, who, barely six months after berating her, were now using her as a cautionary tale against dieting. "[W]hat will be the after-effects of [her] strenuous and painful treatment?" it worried in between warnings and advice from doctors. Perhaps they realized the callousness of their previous jabs: "the producers . . . when they demand a pound of flesh, also demand a part of the life-span of the star; without realizing . . . [they] point the way to the hospital."[33]

While she convalesced at the home she shared with her sister and mother, O'Neil embraced the new "talkie" phenomenon: "[p]etite Sally O'Neil's ability to sing and dance had never been put to any use other than entertaining her family . . . ."[34] and she read publicity for *The Sophomore* (1929), one of eight films she appeared in that year, almost all musically/"backstage" themed. One, *On with the Show!* (1929), was one of the first all-talking films shot completely in color. O'Day joined her for *The Show of Shows* (1929), whose "Meet My Sister" number showcased many of the sister pairs in Hollywood.

The new decade arrived and Molly still wasn't back to full health. She appeared in *Sisters* (1930) with (who else) Sally, but the film received little notice. Both sisters were deep in debt and, after declaring bankruptcy, they toured the Vaudeville circuit to try and recoup some money. Part of that time was with Fanchon and Marco, well-known for "high energy, flashy"[35] musical/dance spectacles bursting with star content, some on the way up (Frances Gumm, a.k.a. Judy Garland, Betty Grable), some down (ahem). By summer 1930, their tour was all but finished.

Molly's career continued to limp along Poverty Row, until an exciting opportunity popped up in 1933: romantic lead for a new Buster Keaton movie. Keaton, alcoholic and unemployable, was approached by Kennedy Films, a fledgling independent film company based in St. Petersburg, Florida. They needed big names; the rock-bottom Keaton needed a comeback. Thrilled with the potential of exploring his old creativity, he signed a deal. The film, tentatively titled *The Fisherman*, was to be directed by our old friend Mickey Neilan, also a heavy drinker on hard times. Shooting was to begin by mid-June. Then, by mid-to-late July. By mid-August, the production was dead, killed by financial constriction, lack of competent off-screen assistance, and hellish conditions:

*Sally and Frank Albertson in* The Brat. Photoplay, *November 1931. Photo courtesy the* Media History Digital Library.

heat and humidity so bad it melted the film in the cameras and the makeup off Molly's face, and gigantic bug swarms (Buster said the mosquitoes "seemed to have teeth"[36]).

Sally's exciting opportunity was much more productive and beneficial. After a few mediocre pictures, including a 1930 remake of the old chestnut *Kathleen Mavourneen*, she slipped on Nazimova's formidable shoes for the talking version of *The Brat* (1931). Legend has it that, after reading the play and falling in love with the "little street waif," she heard the studio had already assigned the role to Maureen O'Sullivan. A visiting priest, a family friend, noticed her weeping and asked why; O'Neil told him

*Molly in* The Life of Vergie Winters. Silver Screen, *September 1934. Photo courtesy the* Media History Digital Library.

everything, including that John Ford was directing. "I know Jack Ford," he replied. "I'm going to have a talk with him."[37] The studio called her in for a screen test the next day, and the part was hers.

A sweet story to be sure, but even sweeter was the five-year 20th Century Fox contract the film's success earned her. A few months later, O'Neil was linked romantically with newly-divorced Arthur Loew, then vice-president of MGM. O'Day spilled the beans: "I know they are engaged to be married, but I believe no date has been set for the wedding."[38] No wedding ever materialized, supposedly due to Sally's career comeback. (Loew remarried someone back east shortly thereafter.)

No romance in the gossip about O'Day, just snide remarks about her wasted talent and current position "linger[ing] on the fringe of the industry . . . [she] made a hit in *The Patent Leather Kid* and then headed for obscurity." They also managed to slip in a comment about her "buxom figure."[39] Molly managed to work steadily for low-budget outfits like Starmark, Reliable, and Pinnacle Productions. *Chloe, Love is Calling You* (1934), Olive Borden's last picture, is particularly cringe-worthy with its terribly racist "voodoo rites" plot. A fresh round of dieting and sacrifice introduced a "slim and lovely"[40] O'Day alongside Ann Harding in *The Life of Vergie Winters* (1934), one of the last movies before true enforcement of The Code.

By December, she was Mrs. Jack Durant of "Mitchell and Durant" fame; their "knockabout" act was popular from Vaudeville through motion pictures, ending in 1938. Durant continued a solo act well into the early 1970s. Molly retired in 1935, her last film being *Skull and Crown*, where she was billed fourth, after Rin Tin Tin Jr. Durant and O'Day had four children; daughter Jacqueline attempted to carry on the family business but only earned one credit, a bit part in the juvenile delinquent exploitation flick *This Rebel Breed* (1960),[41] best known for a pre-West Side Story Rita Moreno.

While Molly cared for her family, Sally lived in New York City.[42] Her sterling 20th Century Fox contract had tarnished quickly; she quit films after *Kathleen* (1938), yet another bargain-basement rehash of *Kathleen Mavourneen*, and headed for the Great White Way and the British comedy *When We Are Married*. Molly joined the cast in late April 1940, replacing a cast member through the show's end on May 4.[43]

After that, aside from O'Neil touring with the USO, we didn't hear much from the Noonan sisters until the 1950s. A year after O'Day and Durant divorced in 1951, she married oilman James Kenaston (whose brother was married to Billie Dove).[44] O'Neil wed manufacturing president Stewart Battles in 1953, gaining three stepchildren.[45] Molly's second and last marriage ended after just four years; she cited Kenaston's cruel and unpredictable behavior as the culprit: "[o]ne time he smashed a raw egg on my head at a dinner party . . . [t]hen on Thanksgiving . . . he gave me a swift kick and my head landed in the oven. . . . "[46] Happily, Sally's was solid and lasted the rest of her life.

Both sisters went into real estate, Sally with sister Isabel and her second husband, realtor Don Cameron.[47] O'Neil and Battles relocated to Galesburg, Illinois sometime in the 1960s, and it was there she died of pneumonia on June 19, 1968. She was 55.[48] Molly remained in California, living in Santa Monica for a while, then moved to Avila Beach in 1980. She devoted her later years to the Old Mission Parish and assisting the homeless. She died in Arroyo Grande on October 15, 1998. She was 88.[49]

1   "Obituary: Mr. Thomas Francis Noonan, Jr." The New Jersey Law Journal, July 1910.

2   "New Jersey, Marriages, 1678-1985," Database, FamilySearch (https://familysearch.org/ark:/61903/1:1:FZGL-MPD:accessed May 14 2015), Thomas F. Noonan and Ann S. Kelly, 25 Jun 1890; citing 495,711.

3   Year: 1910; Census Place: Bayonne Ward 3, Hudson, New Jersey; Roll: T624_886; Page: 9B; Enumeration District: 0019; FHL microfilm: 1374899 Ancestry.com. 1910 United States Federal Census [database on-line]. Provo, UT, USA: Ancestry.com Operations Inc, 2006. Accessed May 13, 2015.

4   "Sally O'Neil." The Three Stooges Online Filmography. n.d. Web. Accessed May 9, 2015. <http://www.threestooges.net/cast/actor/931>

5   Vallance, Tom. "Obituary: Molly O'Day." The Independent (UK), October 28, 1998.

6   Wahl, Jessica. "Miss Molly O'Day." Silence is Platinum, April 20, 2014. Web. Accessed May 10, 2015. <http://silenceisplatinum.blogspot.com/2014/04/miss-molly-oday_20.html>

7   "Jerry Noonan." Wikipedia: The Free Encyclopedia. Wikimedia Foundation, Inc. February 26, 2012.

8   Reid, Margaret. "Found at Last - Sally." Picture Play, June 1926.

9   Ibid.

10  Pardy, George T. "Pre-Release Reviews of Features: Mike." *Motion Picture News*, January 23, 1926.

11  Villecco, Tony (2001). Silent Stars Speak: *Interviews with Twelve Cinema Pioneers.* McFarland and Co. Inc.

12  Pardy, George T. "Sally, Irene and Mary." *Motion Picture News*, December 19, 1925.

13  Hall, Mordaunt. "THE SCREEN: Three Chorus Girls." *New York Times*, December 7, 1925.

14  "The Shadow Stage." *Photoplay*, February 1926.

15  "Dorothy Mackaill Off 1st Nat'l's Payroll." *Variety*, January 12, 1927.

16  Brennan, Lilian W. "A Review of Reviews." *Film Daily*, August 22, 1927.

17  Hall, Mordaunt. "Mr. Barthelmess at His Best." *New York Times*, August 16, 1927.

18  Reid, "Found at Last – Sally."

19  Ibid.

20  Glass, Madeline. "Foiled Again!" *Picture Play*, February 1928.

21  Woolridge, A.L. "Will the Stars Behave?" *Picture Play*, December 1927.

22  Villecco, *Silent Stars Speak.*

23  "'The Lovelorn' at Tower." *Miami Daily News and Metropolis* (FL), October 3, 1928.

24  Schallert, Edwin and Elza. "Hollywood High-Lights." *Picture Play*, December 1927.

25  Wilson, Elizabeth. "Just One More Chance." *Silver Screen*, November 1931.

26  Albert, Katherine. "How Sally Got 'The Brat'." *Photoplay*, November 1931.

27  Shirley, Lois. "Starving Back to Stardom." Photoplay, August 1928.

28  Ibid.

29  "Reduces Weight By Knife." *New York Times*, September 4, 1928.

30  Albert, Katherine. "DIET – The Menace of Hollywood." *Photoplay*, January 1929.

31  Vallance, "Obituary: Molly O'Day."

32  Kingsley, Grace. "Butterflies and Bachelor Boys." *Screenland*, February 1929.

33  Albert, "DIET."

34  "Sally O'Neil Sings and Dances at Savoy." The *Delmarvia Star* (Wilmington, DE), November 24, 1929.

35  Mallory, Mary. "Fanchon and Marco Face the Music and Dance." *Hollywood Heights / The Daily Mirror*, March 3, 2014. Web. Accessed May 10, 2015.

36  Keaton, Buster, with Charles Samuels (1960). *My Wonderful World of Slapstick.* Doubleday.

37  Albert, "How Sally Got 'The Brat'."

38  "Sally O'Neil To Be Married." The *Evening News* (San Jose, CA), April 9, 1932.

39  Glass, Madeline. "One-Day Stars." *Picture Play*, April 1932.

40  "Old Friends." *Silver Screen*, September 1934.

41  "Molly's Daughter." *Toledo Blade* (OH), October 8, 1959.

42  Year: 1940; Census Place: New York, New York, New York; Roll: T627_2643; Page: 81B; Enumeration District: 31-833. Ancestry.com. 1940 United States Federal Census [database on-line]. Provo, UT, USA: Ancestry.com Operations, Inc., 2012. Accessed May 9, 2015.

43   Cohen, Harold W. "The Drama Desk: East and West." *Pittsburg Post-Gazette* (PA), April 24, 1940.

44   "Who's News Today." *Milwaukee Sentinel* (WI), November 14, 1952.

45   "California, County Marriages, 1850-1952," Database with images, FamilySearch (https://familysearch.org/ark:/61903/1:1:K86H-VGF : accessed May 11 2015), Stewart Sedwick Battles and Virginia Louise Noonan, 10 Oct 1953; citing Los Angeles, California, United States, county courthouses, California; FHL microfilm 1,343,364.

46   "Former Actress Awarded Divorce." *Eureka Humboldt Standard* (CA), August 9, 1956.

47   Advertisement in The *Desert Sun* (Palm Springs, CA), May 28, 1960, pg. 13.

48   "Obituary: Sally O'Neil, 55, Ex-Movie Actress." *New York Times*, June 20, 1968.

49   Oliver, Myrna. "Obituary: Molly O'Day; Actress in 'Our Gang' [sic], Films." *Los Angeles Times*, October 21, 1998.

## Other Sources:

Aliperti, Cliff. "The Patent Leather Kid (1927) Starring Richard Barthelmess and Molly O'Day." *Immortal Ephemera*, May13, 2015. Web. Accessed May 14, 2015. < http://immortalephemera.com/59297/the-patent-leather-kid-1927/>

"Brother of Screen Actress Held By Police." *Modesto News-Herald* (CA), April 1, 1932.

Blurbs on the Jack Noonan case from Variety:

-October 20, 1929.
-April 23, 1930.
-April 30, 1930.
-July 16, 1930.
-July 23, 1930.

Douglas, George H. (1999). *The Golden Age of the Newspaper*. Greenwood.

Hayes, Harmony. "I Wonder What's Become of Sally?" *Hollywood*, January 1936.

"Jack Noonan Escapes." *New York Times*, November 4, 1930.

"Jack Noonan Seized Here on Theft Charge." *New York Times*, September 16, 1929.

"Jacquelyn Durant." *IMDb: The Internet Movie Database*. n.d. Web. Accessed May 13, 2015.

*MetOpera Database*. n.d. Web. Accessed May 9, 2015. < http://archives.metoperafamily.org/archives/frame.htm>

Neibaur, James L. (2010). *The Fall of Buster Keaton: His Films for M-G-M, Educational Pictures, and Columbia*. The Scarecrow Press.

S. D., Trav. "Buster Keaton in 'Battling Butler'." *Travalanche*, September 19, 2014. Web. Accessed May 12, 2015. <https://travsd.wordpress.com/2014/09/19/buster-keaton-in-battling-butler/>

S. D., Trav. "Stars of Vaudeville #326: Mitchell and Durant." *Travalanche*, May 20, 2011. Web. Accessed May 12, 2015. <https://travsd.wordpress.com/2011/05/12/stars-of-vaudeville-326-mitchell-and-durant/>

Skip. "Film Reviews: Sally, Irene and Mary." *Variety*, December 9, 1925.

Stewart, Jane. "Am I My Brother's Keeper?" *Modern Screen*, November 1930.

"Talkies in Tabloid: The Brat." *Silver Screen*, November 1931.

Thomas, Dan. "Hollywood." The *Evening Independent* (St Petersburg, FL), October 10, 1927.

"Three Sisters and Brother in 'Lovelorn' Roles." *Sausalito News* (CA), December 17, 1927.

"When We Are Married." *IMDb: The Internet Movie Database*. n.d. Web. Accessed May 13, 2015.

Wollstein, Hans J. *All Movie Guide*. Web. Accessed May 17, 2015.

Special thanks to Laura Wagner and her piece on Molly O'Day, originally posted on her Facebook page, October 17, 2014. Used with permission.

# Chapter 12:
# Mabel and Edith Taliaferro

*Mabel (L) and Edith Taliaferro, Motion Picture News, November 21, 1914. Photos courtesy the Media History Digital Library.*

Many women have laid claim to the title "America's Sweetheart" over the years, but it first gained prominence with the dawn of motion pictures and a charming little actress named . . . if you said "Mary Pickford," you're wrong. Surprised? Then let me introduce you to Mabel Taliaferro. Actually, you should meet her mother first.

Anna Barriscale, a relative of actress Bessie Barriscale, was born in England and emigrated to the US in 1880.[1] She married Robert Taliaferro, a merchant from an august Virginia family, in April (some sources say September or December) 1886.[2] Despite being just nineteen, Anna was no shrinking violet, as evidenced by the "cowhiding" she gave her brother-in-law for both insulting her and "inveigl[ing] her husband into houses of ill- repute."[3] She and Robert had two daughters: Maybelle, born May 21, 1887,[4]

*Edith (L) and Mabel on summer vacation. Theatre Magazine, June 1912. Photo courtesy the Internet Archive.*

and Edith, born December 21, 1894.[5]

By the turn of the century, Anna was a well-established children's theatrical agent, "supplying managers with A1 talent."[6] Parents trusted her, since her own two daughters had been acting since they were each two-and-a-half. After all, Mrs. Taliaferro wouldn't try "to get their children into a trade where she would not have her own."[7] Anna worked incredibly hard to earn that level of respect, and a good reputation was the most important thing in the world.

When the *Morning Telegraph* claimed she and Robert were headed for divorce thanks to her alleged dalliance with boarder G. Stewart Clark, Robert dashed off an incensed letter to the editor: "I have always had implicit confidence in the integrity, virtue and character of my wife . . . it has never occurred to me at any time to cast any reflections upon my wife of any character by divorce court or otherwise."[8] This was carefully crafted to protect Anna's business, nothing more. In reality, while Anna was living in Manhattan with Edith (Maybelle was away at school in New Jersey[9]), Robert was waiting tables, dividing his time between New York City, Long Island, and a woman named Katie.[10] He did not contest Anna's February 1905 divorce suit, and she won full custody of the girls.

Four months later, Anna married James M. Abell,[11] owner and proprietor of the Inn at Long Beach (later renamed Hotel Abell), a sprawling seaside hotel popular with the well-to-do. Within five years Anna was assistant manager. Another year later and, while Edith with her "mind of a girl of 18"[12] was taking a break from the stage for her own schooling, Mabel was actually eighteen and entering full-fledged adulthood.

Both sisters were the darlings of the New York stage since they were toddlers. Brown-haired, hazel-eyed Mabel (spelling simplified) got her start, if you believe the story, quite by accident: she literally tumbled into a reading of *Blue Jeans* while at play. The entire road company fell in love with her and she was immediately cast.[13] From there, she made her official New York debut in 1899's *Children of the Ghetto*, and worked steadily through 1904, where she originated the role of Lovey Mary in *Mrs. Wiggs of the Cabbage Patch*. Critics were impressed with her "exquisite . . . personal grace and artistic skill."[14] (Edith Storey was also in the cast as "Australia.")

Her next play, *You Never Can Tell* (1905), was successful, but *Pippa Passes* (1906) changed her life. Fred Thompson, famous for co-creating Coney Island's Luna Park and the Hippodrome along with Elmer "Skip" Dundy, was in the audience. He had become a theatrical agent, but it wasn't Mabel's performance that piqued his interest. Both Thompson and Mabel vacillated between child and adult, he as the "everyday Peter Pan of New York," she the "veteran player of children and fairies."[15] He sensed not only a kindred spirit, but, as historian Woody Register wrote, the perfect specimen to "indulge, flatter, and promote [his] image."[16]

The two married on November 30, 1906,[17] only two weeks after their engagement. Mabel was barely nineteen, Thompson was thirty-four. The wedding surprised Anna, who didn't find out until the ceremony was over,[18] but given her sharp business acumen I suspect she got over it quickly and approved of the high- profile union. Fred became both her husband and manager, and their first project together was a big one: *Polly of the Circus* (1907-08), a play about an injured circus aerialist forced to choose between loving a minister or letting him go for his career (and propriety)'s sake. Thompson both produced the play and designed the opulent sets, overflowing with big top color and pizzazz. It was an instant hit and made Mabel a star.

Thompson, keenly conscious of his bride's new public image, jumped on every PR opportunity, regardless of reason. Four days

*Mabel as Lovey Mary in Mrs. Wiggs of the Cabbage Patch, with Madge Carr Cook as Mrs. Wiggs and William Burton James as Little Tommy. Theatre Magazine, July 1904. Photo courtesy the Internet Archive.*

*Edith at the time she appeared in* Rebecca of Sunnybrook Farm. Theatre Magazine, *May 1911. Photo courtesy the* Internet Archive.

after *Polly of the Circus* opened, the carriage Fred bought Mabel for Christmas was in a collision. Thompson was unhurt but Mabel suffered bruises and a deep laceration on her left arm. News reports credited Fred's speed and heroism in saving her from serious injury: "[the doctor] said the cut on Miss Taliaferro's arm goes to the bone, but Mr. Thompson's prompt bandaging saved her from losing much blood." Thompson's statement: "[s]he is all right now and will be able to play through every performance. But she is sorry to lose the new brougham, my Christmas present to her."[19]

*Polly of the Circus* closed in May 1908, and the happy couple summered at the Inn, along with Edith, "who soon is to be a full-fledged star."[20] Autumn found Mabel and *Polly of the Circus* on the road, but a November bout of appendicitis sidelined her in Baltimore. Thompson rushed to her side but also made sure the press knew Edith would replace her sister and complete the tour.[21]

1909 brought the Tarkington period piece, *Springtime*, which wilted quickly, despite publicity stunts like letting the audience choose whether Mabel should change her name to "Nell" (a resounding no).[22] Thompson worked her hard and often, packing her little downtime with social appearances like the lavish dinner party he threw at the Hotel Imperial for their third anniversary.[23] It was all like a backdrop from one of their plays: beautiful, vibrant, and completely fake. Before long, it crumpled like one. Mabel collapsed at a 1910 performance of *The Call of the Cricket*, another flop, and the doctor summoned to the Belasco diagnosed "a complete nervous breakdown."[24] Thompson closed the play and insisted he had no idea his wife was so exhausted, but overwork wasn't the only thing breaking Mabel down.

A blazing temper, fueled by alcohol, turned Peter Pan into an abusive shadow. It began, recalled Mabel, in August of 1909 when Thompson "shook her violently."[25] He attacked her three more times throughout 1910, often leaving bruises: "[h]e dragged me across the floor and threw me against the wall and pinched me and twisted my wrist."[26] Mabel left him that September and officially filed for divorce in February 1911. Thompson downplayed things, saying Mabel just preferred to spend time with a friend, but by the time of the final decree in March 1912[27] his image was

*Mabel in* Cinderella. Moving Picture World, *December 2, 1911. Photo courtesy the* Media History Digital Library.

finished. Once devil-may-care, now merely bedeviled, Thompson filed for bankruptcy that same year, and was dead by 1919 due to Bright's Disease and a host of other illnesses.[28]

Dark-haired, rosy-cheeked Edith, meantime, was spending 1910 basking in the most dazzling role of her career: originating the title character in *Rebecca of Sunnybrook Farm*. Reviews for the show were ecstatic: ". . . acted most exquisitely . . . a fairy tale come true." Only the finest praise for Edith's Rebecca, "an acted symphony of childhood . . . as fresh and appealing as Spring itself."[29]

(Also earning notices as "wholly adorable" was future film actress Violet Mersereau.) The mega-hit ran for 216 performances and remained associated with Edith for the rest of her life.

*Rebecca of Sunnybrook Farm* premiered at a time when the Gerry Society was cracking down hard on child performers. Six-teen-year-old Edith vehemently defended her profession: "why doesn't the law leave the stage child alone and get after the ragged little kiddies that sell papers and black boots 'til after mid-night for a few cents a day?"[30] Appearances and reputation were just as important to her mother as to her, and she made sure the public knew she and her sister loved their work and were "healthy as can be."[31] Her reputation took another hit in 1912, when Deane Larabee Weaver, vacationing at Long Beach, wrote his wife that he took "a moonlit ride in an automobile" with Edith. Mrs. Weaver, in a fine bit of overreacting, promptly sued for divorce and pub-licly presented the letter as grounds. Though Weaver apologized and admitted he'd only been joking, Anna sued for $100,000 damaged for "false and defamatory statements." Their lawyers insisted money had nothing to do with it: "[t]he sole purpose . . . was to set her right before the country, where she is known as a young woman with . . . propriety of conduct and purity of char-acter."[32] No word on what the actual settlement was, though the papers noted that on his $5 weekly salary it would take Weaver decades to come anywhere near it.

1911 was a pivotal year for Mabel. Besides the divorce, she took a leap that no actor in the U.S. had yet dared to attempt: legiti-mate theater to motion pictures. Someone with her stage reputa-tion going to the vastly inferior "flickers" was highly unusual, and so Mabel was heralded into films with pomp and fanfare second only to Bernhardt's. "Into the motion picture firmament has come a new star . . ." trumpeted columnist C. Wirt Adams. "[O]ut of the fullness of continuous and brilliant success on the legitimate stage, Mabel Taliaferro has stepped lightly into the daintiest, sweetest and loveliest of pictures."[33] He was talking about Selig's super-production of *Cinderella* (1912), the perfect vehicle for her.

Dainty, sweet, and lovely: Mabel was perpetually described as such, as if she never grew beyond childhood. Her sister wasn't immune either; *Picture Play* said they were both the go-to ladies for "slender girlishness and charm."[34] *Cinderella* had been filmed before, and was a staple on the stage, but no one threw money at it like Selig, expanding the story to a lavish three-reel affair "of extraordinary qualities . . . such dramatic fullness that in no part could it be reduced by so much as a yard of film."[35] The drama also starred Winifred Greenwood as Cinderella's mother, Frank Weed as her father, and Thomas J. Carrigan as Prince Charming. The prestige picture was released as a holiday gift to audiences on New Year's Day 1912.

Six months later, while in Canada, Edith married Thomas Earle Brown.[36] He acted and directed under his professional name of Earle Browne, but was better-known for writing; he later contributed to the Babe Ruth vehicle, *Headin' Home* (1920), *The Love of Sunya* (1927) with Gloria Swanson, and John Barrymore's lauded *Sherlock Holmes* (1922). The two met when Edith subbed for a sick Mabel in *Polly of the Circus* back in 1908. Directly after their marriage, Edith took temporary leave from the stage.

Would Mabel be bitten again by the marriage bug? "What I am going to do concerns me alone,"[37] she coyly remarked, but Cinderella wasn't immune to Prince Charming: she and Thomas Carrigan wed on June 1, 1913.[38] The ceremony was held in the Michigan woods, with only her mother and "two brothers"[39] (most likely Carrigan's) attending. The two managed to keep it secret until local dispatches broke the story a month later.

After her stellar start in movies, Mabel appeared in thirteen more—first with Selig, then with Metro—through 1917. Mabel's films were all squeaky clean, featuring the same darling prepubescent she'd perfected on the stage. Infatuated audiences crowned her "Sweetheart of the American Movies." Two films with meatier credentials were directed by Tod Browning (of *Freaks* fame). In *Peggy, the Will O' the Wisp* (1917), she stretched her comedy muscles, playing a Robin Hood-style highwayman stealing from the rich to help a peasant's wife get medical care (no insurance then). She demonstrated skill in horseback riding and elevated the scant source material; "her vitality and prettiness count wonders . . . it is only to be regretted that she was not provided with

*Edith and Jack Sherrill in* The Conquest of Canaan. Motography, *September 9, 1916. Photo courtesy the Media History Digital Library.*

a vehicle more worthy."[40] Carrigan joined her as Peggy's sweetheart. In *The Jury of Fate* (1917), she played twins: well-behaved Jeanne and her spoiled brother Jacques, their father's favorite. When Jacques accidentally drowns, Jeanne cuts off her hair and dons her brother's clothes to fool Father into thinking it was she who died. She keeps up the deception until her father's own death, at which time she travels to Montreal to find a new life and happiness. Reviews were mixed, and the dark overtones, so much a trademark of Browning, struck audiences as "draggy and morbid."[41] Still, Mabel earned accolades for her "ability to play the beloved waif girl . . . second only to Mae Marsh."[42] (When *Polly of the Circus* hit screens in 1917, it was Marsh, rather than either Taliaferro, cast in the title role.)

Edith signed her own movie contract with Lasky in October 1914[43] just after finishing *Tipping the Winner* on Broadway. Back in January, Mabel had joined her for *Young Wisdom*, and critics were thrilled with the sisters' new maturity, Mabel "infusing a spicy flavor" into her typical "passive sweetness," Edith exhibiting "pathos [and] strength of emotion never before suspected."[44] Edith's screen career, however, would prove incredibly brief, spanning only three films: a shop girl longing for the life of the social elite in William C. deMille's "sparkling, exuberant"[45] comedy *Young Romance* (1915); the mediocre film adaptation of Booth Tarkington's *The Conquest of Canaan* (1916), where her acting was called "stagy;"[46] and *Who's Your Brother* (1919), sold as documenting the struggles of soldiers returning to a post-war world but really a typical romance, albeit one where Edith "seem[ed] to play the part with sincerity."[47]

Afterwards she was content to remain in the "legitimate" theater, particularly after the giant hit, *Captain Kidd Jr.*, in 1916, and intermittently continued through *The Hook-Up* in 1935. By this time, she was divorced from Browne and married to actor House Jameson,[48] best-known for his long run on NBC's radio and television sitcom *The Aldrich Family*. They would remain married until Edith's death on March 2, 1958, after a long illness. She was 64.[49]

Mabel's output dwindled after 1917, with only four more films before she left to focus on the stage, although she did make a small comeback in *My Love Came Back* (1940) with Olivia deHavilland. She and Carrigan, who had one son together, divorced in May 1919;[50] she married Captain Joseph O'Brien eight months later.[51] They relocated to a farm in Stamford Connecticut, where Mabel's son William went missing; after a large search effort, the two-and-a-half year old was discovered in the woods, exhausted but thankfully unhurt.[52] Wedded bliss ended yet again for Mabel by 1927, when she sued O'Brien, now a continuity writer in Hollywood, for intolerable cruelty.[53] O'Brien countersued on the grounds of desertion.[54] The divorce was final by 1929,[55] and in her revolving door fashion Mabel and William were living with actor/director Robert Ober by 1930.[56] The two were commonly referred to as married, and the relationship lasted until Ober's death in 1950.[57]

Mabel and Ober stayed active on the stage, in everything from Broadway to local summer stock, even attempting one of Ober's own plays, *Ann Adams, Spinster* (1933), to poor reviews.[58] After his death, Mabel then found work in television, performing in several teleplays, as well as a featured role on WPIX's *Leave it to Papa*, a 1951 sitcom about "Italian family life."[59] Her last TV appearance was in 1956 on *The Joseph Cotten Show*. Mabel, honored with a star on the Hollywood Walk of Fame in 1960, spent her later years happily retired in Hawaii. She died in Honolulu, aged 91, on January 24, 1979.[60] During her last Broadway success, the 1944 musical *Bloomer Girl*, journalist Robert Francis asked her what advice she could give to young newcomers: "[t]here will always be a lot of youngsters who will smash their way in . . . it's in their blood and they've got what it takes for success . . . that kind never asks for advice. They don't have to."[61]

1 "New York, Passenger Lists, 1820-1891," database with images, FamilySearch (https://familysearch.org/ark:/61903/1:1:QVSK-PD1W : accessed April 7, 2015), Anna Barriscole, 1880; citing NARA microfilm publication M237 (Washington, D.C.: National Archives and Records Administration, n.d.); FHL microfilm.

2 "New York, Marriages, 1686-1980," database, FamilySearch (https://familysearch. org/ark:/61903/1:1:F6WD-TMD: accessed April 6, 2015), Robert B. Taliaferro and Annie Barriscale, 05 Apr 1886; citing reference ; FHL microfilm 1,570,948.

3 "A Jacksonville Sensation." The *Daily Saratogan* (Saratoga Springs, NY), January 6, 1888.

4 Number: 086-09-3122; Issue State: New York; Issue Date: Before 1951 Ancestry.com. U.S., Social Security Death Index, 1935-2014 [database on-line]. Provo, UT, USA: Ancestry.com Operations Inc, 2011.

5 National Archives and Records Administration; Washington, D.C.; Manifests of Passengers Arriving in the St. Albans, Vermont, District through Canadian Pacific Ports, 1929-1949; National Archives Microfilm Publication: M1465; Record Group Title: Records of the Immigration and Naturalization Service Ancestry.com. U.S., Border Crossings from Canada to U.S., 1895-1956 [database on-line]. Provo, UT, USA: Ancestry.com Operations, Inc., 2010.

6 Advertisement in The *New York Dramatic Mirror*, August 18, 1900, pg. 24.

7   "Where Children Are Chosen For Positions On The Stage." *New York Times*, April 17, 1904.

8   "Taliaferros Deny It." The *New York Morning Telegraph*, June 17, 1900.

9   Year: 1900; Census Place: Ridgefield, Bergen, New Jersey; Roll: 954; Page: 20B; Enumeration District:0004; FHL microfilm: 1240954. Ancestry.com. 1900 United States Federal Census [database on-line]. Provo, UT, USA: Ancestry.com Operations Inc, 2004.

10  "Divorce Suits Undefended." The *Brooklyn Daily Eagle*, February 26, 1905.

11  Ancestry.com. New York, New York, Marriage Index 1866-1937 [database on-line]. Provo, UT, USA: Ancestry.com Operations, Inc., 2014. Original data: Index to New York City Marriages, 1866-1937. Indices prepared by the Italian Genealogical Group and the German Genealogy Group, and used with permission of the New York City Department of Records/Municipal Archives.

12  Josaphare, Lionel. "From Stage to School: That is Edith's Plan." The *Brooklyn Daily Eagle*, March 12, 1905.

13  Montayne, Lillian. "As They Grew Up." *Motion Picture*, October 1917.

14  "'Mrs. Wiggs' in Drama Is Now At The Savoy." *New York Times*, September 4, 1904.

15  Register, Woody (2003). *The Kid of Coney Island: Fred Thompson and the Rise of American Amusements*. Oxford U. Press.

16  Ibid.

17  "New York, New York City Marriage Records, 1829-1940," database, FamilySearch (https://familysearch.org/ark:/61903/1:1:249D-G7T : accessed April 9, 2015), Fredrick Thompson and Mabel Taliaferro, 30 Nov 1906; citing Marriage, Manhattan, New York, New York, United States, New York City Municipal Archives, New York; FHL microfilm.

18  "Fred Thompson Marries." *New York Times*, December 1, 1906.

19  "Mabel Taliaferro Hurt in Car Crash." *New York Times*, December 27, 1907.

20  "Long Beach Lively." *New York Times*, July 12, 1908.

21  "Mabel Taliaferro Ill." *New York Times*, November 16, 1908.

22  "Miss Taliaferro Drops Nell." *New York Times*, October 31, 1909.

23  "The Thompsons Celebrate." *New York Times*, December 1, 1909.

24  "Mabel Taliaferro Suffers Collapse." *New York Times*, May 5, 1910.

25  "Mabel Taliaferro Sues." *New York Times*, December 3, 1911.

26  Register, The Kid of Coney Island.

27  "Mabel Taliaferro Divorced." *New York Times*, March 17, 1912.

28  "Frederic Thompson, Show Builder, Dies." *New York Times*, June 7, 1919.

29  "The Heart of a Child in This Tender Play." *New York Times*, October 4, 1910.

30  "Children On the Stage." *New York Times*, July 31, 1910.

31  Ibid.

32  "Actress Sues Boaster." *New York Tribune*, November 3, 1912.

33  Adams, C. Wirt. "Mabel Taliaferro as Cinderella." *Motography*, December 1911.

34  "Mabel Taliaferro." *Picture Play*, August 1916.

35  Adams, "Mabel Taliaferro as Cinderella."

36  "Ontario Marriages, 1869-1927," database with images, FamilySearch (https://familysearch.org/ark:/61903/1:1:KS88- YZX : accessed April 2, 2015), Thomas Earle Browne and Edith Tolliver, 04 Jun 1912; citing registration , Toronto, York, Ontario, Canada, Archives of Ontario, Toronto; FHL microfilm.

37  "Mabel Taliaferro Divorced." *New York Times*.

38  "Michigan, Marriages, 1868-1925," database with images, FamilySearch (https://familysearch.org/ark:/61903/1:1:N3LH-4VW : accessed April 2, 2015), Thomas J. Carrigan and Mabel E. Taliaferro, 01 Jun 1913; citing Lapeer, Lapeer, Michigan, v 3 p 5 rn 1364, Department of Vital Records, Lansing; FHL microfilm 2,342,701.

39  "Mabel Taliaferro a Bride." *New York Times*, July 10, 1913.

40  Milne, Peter. "Screen Examinations: 'Peggy, the Will O' The Wisp.'" *Motion Picture News*, August 4, 1917.

41  "The Jury of Fate." *Motography*, November 17, 1917.

42  Johnson, Julian. "The Shadow Stage." *Photoplay*, November 1916.

43  "Edith Taliaferro With Lasky." *Moving Picture World*, October 31, 1914.

44  Patterson, Ada. "The Taliaferros – Sisters and Co-Stars." *Theatre Magazine*, February 1914.

45  Bush, W. Stephen. "Young Romance." *Moving Picture World*, February 6, 1915.

46  Bush, W. Stephen. "The Conquest of Canaan." *Moving Picture World*, October 14, 1916.

47  "Clean and Wholesome Story Contains Nothing Unusual But Will Please." *Film Daily*, October 19, 1919.

48  Walters, Larry. "Father Aldrich in Harem Class; Has 4 TV Wives." *Chicago Daily Tribune*, March 14, 1953.

49  "Edith Taliaferro of Stage, Was 64." *New York Times*, March 3, 1958.

50  "Mabel Taliaferro Sued for Divorce." *New York Times*, June 2, 1929.

51  Ibid.

52  "Actress's [sic] Baby Wanders." *New York Times*, January 6, 1921.

53  "Miss Taliaferro Asks Divorce For Cruelty." *New York Times*, December 29, 1927.

54  "Taliaferro Divorce To Be Heard Today." *New York Times*, June 3, 1929.

55  "Mabel Taliaferro Divorced." *New York Times*, June 4, 1929.

56  Year: 1930; Census Place: Los Angeles, Los Angeles, California; Roll: 134; Page: 14A; Enumeration District:0073; Image: 843.0; FHL microfilm: 2339869 Ancestry.com. 1930 United States Federal Census [database on-line]. Provo, UT, USA: Ancestry.com Operations Inc, 2002.

57  "Robert Ober Dies; Veteran Actor, 69." *New York Times*, December 8, 1950.

58  "The Play: Robert Ober and Mabel Taliaferro in 'Ann Adams, Spinster,' at the Sutton Theatre." *New York Times*, March 27, 1933.

59  Lohman, Sidney. "News and Notes of Television and Radio." *New York Times*, December 2, 1951.

60  "Mabel Taliaferro, 91, Star of Silent Screen Acted in 100 Plays." *New York Times*, February 3, 1979.

61  Francis, Robert. "Candid Close-Ups: Mabel Taliaferro of 'Bloomer Girl' Gives Advice to the Youngsters." The *Brooklyn Daily Eagle*, December 10, 1944.

## Other Sources:

"Chicago Amusements by Our Chicago Correspondent." *The Billboard*, September 19, 1908.

"Earle Browne." *IMDb – The Internet Movie Database*. Web. Accessed April 4, 2015.

<http://www.imdb.com/name/nm0114991/>

"Edith Taliaferro." Find A Grave. Web. Accessed April 5, 2015. <http://www.findagrave.com/cgi- bin/fg.cgi?page=gr&GRid=8715771>

"Edith Taliaferro." *IBDb – The Internet Broadway Database*. Web. Accessed April 2, 2015. <http://www.ibdb.com/person.php?id=68860>

Fiore, Roberta, Carole Shahda Geraci, and Dave Roochvarg for the Long Beach Historical Preservation Society (2010). *Long Beach (Images of America Series)*. Arcadia Publishing.

Fisher, James, and Felicia Hardison Londré (2009). *The A to Z of American Theater: Modernism (The A to Z Guide Series)*. Scarecrow Press.

"Frederic Thompson and Elmer 'Skip' Dundy." *PBS American Experience: Coney Island*. Web. Accessed April 7, 2015.<http://www.pbs.org/wgbh/amex/coney/peopleevents/pande01.html>

Hischak, Thomas S. (2003). *Enter the Players: New York Stage Actors in the Twentieth Century*. Scarecrow Press.

"In Philadelphia Theatres." *The New York Dramatic Mirror*, October 16, 1909.

"Mabel Taliaferro Keeps Her Marriage Secret." The *Pittsburg Press* (PA), July 10, 1913.

"Mabel Taliaferro." *Hollywood Walk of Fame*. Web. Accessed April 4, 2015. <http://www.walkoffame.com/mabel- taliaferro>

"Mabel Taliaferro." *IBDb – The Internet Broadway Database*. Web. Accessed April 2, 2015. <http://www.ibdb.com/person.php?id=61796>

"Obituary: Thomas J. Carrigan." New York Times, October 3, 1941.

Shreve, Ivan G., Jr. "Happy Birthday, House Jameson!" *RadioSpirits*. Web. Accessed April 9, 2015. <http://www.radiospirits.info/2013/12/17/happy-birthday-house-jameson/>

Year: 1930; Census Place: Manhattan, New York, New York; Roll: 1562; Page: 1A; Enumeration District: 0627; Image: 409.0; FHL microfilm: 2341297. Ancestry.com. 1930 United States Federal Census [database on-line]. Provo, UT, USA: Ancestry.com Operations Inc, 2002.

# Chapter 13:
## Olive and Alma Tell

*Olive (L) and Alma Tell,* Who's Who on the Screen, *1920. Photo courtesy the Media History Digital Library.*

"Being a direct descendant of the most famous archer the world has ever known," began the article, "it was not strange when Miss Tell decided to shoot her arrow . . . it landed exactly where she *intended.*"[1] So witty, so clever, so patently untrue. Even with early records being notoriously tricky and full of holes, there is more than enough evidence to suggest Alma and Olive Tell weren't Tells at all, but Manahans.

Jeannette Mulry, the lovely young daughter of affluent contractor/ real estate dealer James Mulry, wed John A. Manahan in 1886 under stressful circumstances: her mother was gravely ill and begged her eldest girl to marry at her bedside. Manahan seemed a good catch, a "successful young businessman"[2] with the Cunard steamship line, and the newlyweds, blessed by Mrs. Mulry's miraculous recovery, began married life in the brownstone gifted by Mr. Mulry.

John and Jeannette had four daughters: Ethel (1890), Mercedes (1891), Genevieve (1894), and J. Ursula (1896).[3] The marriage was fruitful but definitely not blissful. By the time of her father's death in April 1897, while visiting his estates in Ireland (including Castle Strange, about 95 miles from Dublin), Jeannette already had ample evidence of John's infidelity. Distraught and reluctant to bring divorce charges due to her devout Catholic upbringing, she eventually filed, "forced to take the step . . . on behalf of her self [sic] and children."[4] Courts ruled in her favor largely due to eyewitness testimony from various parties, including private detectives, of John's "intimacy with a woman at the Delaware Hotel."[5] Jeannette was awarded custody of all four girls and $2000 a year alimony. John refused to pay, saying she'd inherited more than enough from her father's estate—and he knew, since he'd managed it. The case dragged on for more than two years until Manahan was arrested for contempt and required to pay monies owed.[6]

The Manahan girls flourished in the upper class environment Jeannette provided. All three (Mercedes, the second oldest, died suddenly at age twelve in 1903[7]) received private school education, their home employed a housekeeper and cook,[8] and they and their mother regularly summered in upstate New York at the luxury resorts in the Catskills.[9]

In December 1901, Jeannette quietly married lumberman Laurence Carroll,[10] but her beloved Catholic Church did not recognize her Episcopalian second marriage and refused her the sacraments. So, after six years and one son, Laurence Jr., they separated. It was, as one daughter put it, "simply a case of her love of God being more than that for man."[11] With Ethel having married in 1913, Jeannette lived with Genevieve and J. Ursula in self-imposed exile until her death six years later. She and Carroll remained in love with each other and he was present at her deathbed.

Now here's where things get interesting. In March 1914, two young ladies named Alma and Olive Tell graduated from the American Academy of Dramatic Arts.[12] The prestigious acting school still operated as of 2016 and counted numerous successful alumni, from Edward G. Robinson and Warren William to Adrien Brody and Sarah Paulson. The New York Times, in a society col-

*Olive around the time of her first film. Motion Picture News, March 23, 1918.*
*Photo courtesy the Media History Digital Library.*

umn that June, reported a "Mrs. Janette Tell" and "Miss Olive Tell" stayed at the Hotel Aspenwall in Massachusetts.[13]

In 1919, upon Jeannette's death, her obituary listed "Jeannette Tell Carroll" as the "adored mother of Ethel Moore, Olive Tell,

Alma Tell, and Laurence F. Carroll Jr."[14] Another telling (pun intended) nugget: in a 1921 piece on the Tell sisters, The *Brooklyn Daily Eagle* reported the girls entered the AADA after tiring of their visit at their "grandfather's home, a few miles from Dublin."[15] This combined with Alma's 1932 marriage certificate listing "Janette Mulry" and "J. A. Manahan" as her parents,[16] makes the theory more than plausible that Genevieve and J. Ursula Manahan were Olive and Alma Tell.

Right after graduating, Olive took to the stage, first in stock and then Broadway.[17] She appeared in *Cousin Lucy* (1915) with Julian Eltinge, leaving after two weeks for *Husband and Wife*. Her aplomb in the latter led to the lead in *The Intruder* (1916), but it only lasted a few performances. In between this and the successful *General Post* (1918), she appeared in her first motion picture.

"*The Silent Master*. . . brings to projection the shadow of Olive Tell, a supremely beautiful young woman of the speaking stage."[18] The romantic adventure of the Paris Apache dancers, a popular early theme, featured Olive as the "ideal leading woman in every sense of the word."[19] *The Silent Master* (1917) is considered her screen debut; some sources list *The Smugglers* (1916), but it remains unclear if Mrs. Watts was played by Olive or Alma. That comedy of errors about genuine vs. phony pearls was "unusual in its general excellence"[20] and earned an "exceedingly good"[21] rating for the entire cast.

Alma went straight from school into *Peg O' My Heart* (1914) at the Manhattan Opera House,[22] then stock in Pennsylvania and Maine. Her first film was *Simon, the Jester* (1915), based on the novel by William Locke. When told he has six months to live, wealthy Simon (Edwin Arden) decides to dump his wealth and prestige and focus on helping as many people as he can. He also dumps his fiancée (Tell), who is convinced he has a screw loose. An imbroglio with Lola, the Cat Queen of the Hippodrome and her ilk, livens the plot immensely. Critics praised Alma and the rest of the cast for "capably suppport[ing]" Arden.[23]

From 1917-1921, both ladies were featured on the screen, with Olive edging out her sister in both quantity and promotion. Alma appeared in five pictures, getting pleasant (if indifferent) reviews.

*Olive (L) and John Sunderland in* To Hell With the Kaiser! *Picture Play, December 1918. Photo courtesy the Media History Digital Library.*

In *On With the Dance* and *The Right to Love* (both 1920), she played opposite David Powell, refined stage actor turned "faultless photoplay leading man and adorable villain."[24] Her icy society ladies in both might have been too chilly; some found her "shining"[25] with "beauty and refinement"[26] but most were repelled by her "cold impassiveness"[27] and "goody-goody interpretation."[28] To be fair, both films starred The Girl with the Bee-Stung Lips herself, Mae Murray; against such histrionic competition, any actress was doomed to inferiority.

Olive, meanwhile, appeared in twelve pictures, three of them (*The Unforseen, Her Sister* (both 1917), *The Girl and the Judge* (1918)) also with David Powell, but the magazines truly came calling after *To Hell With the Kaiser!* (1917), eager to interview "the little heroine who has been captivating hearts right and left."[29] Olive, "so small and big eyed and pink and white . . ."[30] happily derailed the standard fluff questions on clothes and cosmetics with ardent remarks on politics, particularly women's suffrage, or exercise. She never considered herself an athlete but she swam,

*From L to R: Martha Mansfield, Edmund Lowe, and Alma in* The Silent Command. Exhibitors Herald, *September 29, 1923. Photo courtesy the* Media History Digital Library.

skated, golfed, and rose horseback regularly. "Where are the old women today?" she smirked. "I'll tell you. They do not exist. This is because they do the things that used to be denied them."[31] Film work initially overwhelmed her, like "a puppy that is just learning to swim must feel when he is thrown into deep water,"[32] but what emerged was "one of the most charming personalities of the theatrical world."[33]

As the Roaring Twenties progressed, the stage was still a second home. *Whispering Wires* (1922-23) was a particular success, running at the Forty-Ninth Street Theatre for 352 performances.[34] Olive continued to decorate the silver screen, in smaller roles like Mrs. Rice in Norma Shearer's first talkie, *The Trial of Mary Dugan* (1929). She also decorated the arm of Kansas City insurance broker George Kroh. The two married April 2, 1922, but their life together was over before it could start; on August 17, 1923,[35] while Olive was in New York appearing in *Morphia*, Kroh died in North Carolina of pulmonary tuberculosis.[36] (He did not die in WWI, as some reports erroneously suggest.) Three years later, Olive found love again with First National producer Henry Hobart, whom she met while making *The Wrong Woman* back in1920.[37] She became the right woman on December 23, 1926.[38] "I couldn't bear to have our life together be staid," she told reporters. "Henry will pretend he is only visiting me. Marriage and love are two things in which the illusions should be preserved." The lovebirds were onto something – their marriage lasted until her death. "I would much rather have one kiss than dozens of roses," she remarked. "It often means more."[39]

Alma appeared in only a handful of films though the 1920s, but *The Silent Command* (1923) deserves special mention. Not only was it a "hectic tale of intrigue"[40] so in love with the U.S. Navy that *Variety* complained it "smack[ed] too much of propaganda,"[41] not only did it feature "really wonderful bits of storm photography,"[42] it was also the American film debut of Bela Lugosi, and one of the final roles of ill-fated actress Martha Mansfield, burned to death only a year later at age twenty-four.

Then there was the time Olive became a criminal. (What would Jeannette say?!) She and eight other cast members were arrested for indecency right before the final act of *The Captive*, at Los Angeles' Mayan Theater.[43] Edouard Bourdet's drama already possessed a salacious reputation by its 1928 West Coast performance. Debuting in New York City in September 1926, the play "about a woman struggling against her passion for another woman"[44] immediately polarized the public. Critics marveled at the intelligent handling of such a mature theme: Brooks Atkinson found it "somber" yet refreshing; Alexander Woolcott felt it "unprecedented;" George Jean Nathan called it "profoundly wrought."[45]

However, average folks—most of whom never even saw the play—sent a clarion call through Manhattan: shut it down! Mayor Walker threatened censorship if *The Captive* (and other shows of similar subject matter) didn't "clean stage."[46] Refusing to change, the show was raided and its actors, including principals Helen Mencken and Basil Rathbone, arrested. The show suffered constant legal action, particularly by the Society for the Suppression of Vice, until it closed in March 1927. New York State law declared a month later that anyone who "presents or participates in any obscene, indecent, criminal or impure" production would be committing a misdemeanor. (It was later amended to exclude ac-

*William Powell and Olive in* Ladies' Man. Photoplay, *May 1931. Photo courtesy the* Media History Digital Library.

tors.[47]) The taboo against *The Captive* reached far beyond New York, hence the reception in California.

"You can't imagine a better woman for the part . . . [s]he is smooth as velvet [and] quite a finished actress."[48] So said a review for *Lawful Larceny* (1930), one of a number of pre-Codes in which Olive popped up. You can find her in *Ten Cents a Dance, Ladies' Man, Devotion, The Right of Way*, and *Delicious*—and that was only 1931! Her most visible role today is Princess Johanna, mother to Marlene Dietrich, in *The Scarlet Empress* (1934).

Alma only appeared in two films in the 1930s, *Love Comes Along* (1930) and an unaccredited role in the acclaimed first version of *Imitation of Life* (1934). In between the two, on December 18, 1932,[49] she became the wife of B-actor Stanley Blystone, best-known today for his frequent work with The Three Stooges. She left the Beverly Hills home she shared with Olive, Hobart, and his children from his first marriage (two doors down from Olive Borden and her mother Sibbie[50]) and retired to Los Angeles with her new husband. On December 29, 1937, Alma died suddenly of a heart attack.[51] Reports gave her age as 39.

Olive kept working through the 1930s, notably appearing in the Shirley Temple vehicle, *Baby Take a Bow* (1934). Her final role was an unaccredited one, in *Zaza* (1938) starring Claudette Colbert.

*A saucy looking Alma.* Exhibitors Trade Review, *November 3, 1923. Photo courtesy the* Media History Digital Library.

By WWII the couple was happily retired and living at The Dryden Hotel on East 39th Street in New York City. One day at home, Olive tripped and fell, fracturing her skull. She died at Bellevue Hospital the next day, June 8, 1951. Her age was reported as 55.[52]

1   Underhill, Harriette. "Olive Tells Her Secrets." *Photoplay*, February 1918.

2   "Hymeneal: Manahan-Mulry." The Long Island City Star (NY), December 14, 1886.

3   "United States Census, 1900," database with images, FamilySearch (https://familysearch.org/ark:/61903/1:1:MSNZ-2SZ:accessed June 12, 2015), Mercedes

Manahan in household of Jane Manahan, Borough of Brooklyn, Election District 23 New York City Ward 23, Kings, New York, United States; citing sheet 3B, family 47, NARA microfilm publication T623 (Washington, D.C.: National Archives and Records Administration, n.d.); FHL microfilm 1,241,061.

4   "Absolute Divorce for Mrs. Manahan." *New York Herald*, June 12, 1898.

5   "Mrs. Manahan Gets Her Divorce." *The Sun* (NY), June 12, 1898.

6   "John A. Manahan Arrested." *New York Times*, October 17, 1900.

7   "Obituary: Manahan." *New York Times*, May 17, 1903.

8   New York, State Census, 1905, database with images, FamilySearch(https://family-search.org/ark:/61903/1:1:SPF8-1VR : accessed June 12, 2015), Genevive Manahan in household of Jeannette Manahan, Manhattan, A.D. 21, E.D. 47, New York, New York; citing p. 61, line 44, county offices, New York.; FHL microfilm 1,433,097.

9   "Catskill Resorts Report Unusually Good Season." *New York Times*, July 26, 1903.

10   Historical Society of Pennsylvania; Philadelphia, Pennsylvania; Collection Name: Historic Pennsylvania Church and Town Records; Reel: 776. Ancestry.com. Pennsylvania and New Jersey, Church and Town Records, 1708-1985 [database on-line]. Provo, UT, USA: Ancestry.com Operations, Inc., 2011. Accessed June 10, 2015.

11   "Her Death Reveals Secret Marriage." *The Sun* (NY), July 10, 1919.

12   "Miss Bates Tells How To Beat Movies." *New York Times*, March 14, 1914.

13   "May Combine Lenox Clubs." *New York Times*, June 22, 1914.

14   "Obituary: Tell." *New York Times*, July 11, 1919.

15   "Olive Tell Is Irish." *The Brooklyn Daily Eagle*, February 13, 1921.

16   "California, County Marriages, 1850-1952," database with images, FamilySearch(https://familysearch.org/ark:/61903/1:1:K8JH-B6D : accessed June 9, 2015), William S Blystone and Alma Tell, 18 Dec 1932; citing Los Angeles, California, United States, county courthouses, California; FHL microfilm 2,075,036.

17   "Olive Tell's Rise." *New York Times*, January 6, 1918.

18   Johnson, Julian. "The Shadow Stage." *Photoplay*, August 1917.

19   "Olive Tell in 'The Silent Master'." *Moving Picture World*, April 21, 1917.

20   Jolo. "Film Reviews: 'The Smugglers'." Variety, July 14, 1916.

21   "Supported by Good Cast." *Marion County Tocsin* (CA), November 18, 1916.

22   "Alma Tell, Actress On Stage and Screen." *New York Times*, January 1, 1938.

23   Thew, Harvey F. "Simon the Jester." *Motion Picture News*, September 25, 1915.

24   Johnson, Julian. "Powell, The Military Heart-Burglar." *Photoplay*, June 1917.

25   Smith, Frederick James. "The Celluloid Critic." *Motion Picture Classic*, April-May 1920.

26   "Extravagant and Spicy: A Sure Winner in Cosmopolitan Houses." *Film Daily*, February 15, 1920.

27   Kelley, Joseph L. "The Right to Love." *Motion Picture News*, September 4, 1920.

28   Naylor, Hazel Simpson. "Across the Silversheet." *Motion Picture*, July 1920.

29   Howe, Selma. "That Very Busy Girl." *Picture Play*, December 1918.

30   Underhill, "Olive Tells Her Secrets."

31   Ibid.

32   Howe, "That Very Busy Girl."

33   "Olive Tell." *Moving Picture World*, September 8, 1917.

34   "Olive Tell." *IBDb - The Internet Broadway Database*. Web. Accessed June 21, 2015. <http://www.ibdb.com/person.php?id=62006>

35   "Obituary: George W. Kroh." *New York Times*, August 19, 1923.

36   "North Carolina, Deaths, 1906-1930," database with images, FamilySearch(https://familysearch.org/ark:/61903/1:1:F384- LJV : accessed June 3, 2015), George W. Kroh, 17 Aug 1923; citing Biltmore, Buncombe, N.C., reference fn 793 it2cd8147cn209, State Department of Archives and History, Raleigh; FHL microfilm 1,893,178.

37   "Actress Weds in Novel Way." *St. Petersburg Times* (FL), December 26, 1926.

38   "Olive Tell Marries Henry Morgan Hobart." *New York Times*, December 24, 1926.

39   "Actress Weds in Novel Way." *St. Petersburg Times*.

40   "Comment On Other Productions." *Motion Picture*, December 1923.

41   "Not Much Novelty in Loop Theatres." *Variety*, September 13, 1923.

42   Johnson, Julian. "The Shadow Stage." *Photoplay*, November 1923.

43   "Stop Play, Arrest Cast." *New York Times*, March 25, 1928.

44   Wilson, Victoria (2013). *A Life of Barbara Stanwyck: Steel-True 1907-1940*. Simon & Schuster.

45   Ibid.

46   "Mayor Starts War On Immoral Plays." *New York Times*, December 29, 1926.

47   *Laws of the State of New York* (Albany: J.B. Lyon, 1927), pg. 1731-32. Amended in September 1931 to exclude musicians and actors.

48   Lee, Nancy. "Reviewing the Screen." *The Milwaukee Journal* (WI), July 13, 1930.

49   "Alma Tell, Actress, Wed." *New York Times*, December 19, 1932.

50   "United States Census, 1930," database with images, FamilySearch(https://familysearch.org/ark:/61903/1:1:XCFF-8LR:accessed June 17, 2015), Alma Tell in household of Henry M Hobart, Beverly Hills, Los Angeles, California, United States; citing enumeration district (ED) 0830, sheet 15B, family 512, line 88, NARA microfilm publication T626 (Washington D.C.: National Archives and Records Administration, 2002), roll 124; FHL microfilm 2,339,859.

51   "Alma Tell." *New York Times*.

52   "Olive Tell, Appeared On Stage and Screen." *New York Times*, June 9, 1951.

## Other Sources:

Ankerich, Michael G. (2011). *Dangerous Curves Atop Hollywood Heels: The Lives, Careers, and Misfortunes of 14 Hard- Luck Girls of the Silent Screen*. BearManor Media.

"August Rush to Catskills." *New York Times*, August 9, 1903.

Blaisdell, George. "The Smugglers." *Moving Picture World*, July 22, 1916.

"Current Releases Reviewed." *Motography*, July 22, 1916.

Denig, Lynde. "Simon, the Jester." *Moving Picture World*, September 25, 1915.

"New York Times: Reaction to 'The Captive,' 1926-1927." *OutHistory*. n.d. Web. Accessed May 20, 2015.

<http://outhistory.org/oldwiki/New_York_Times:_Reaction_to_%22The_Captive%22,_1926-1927>

"Princess Theatre." *Sausalito News* (CA), October 6, 1917.

"Stanley Blystone." *The Three Stooges Online Filmography*. n.d. Web. Accessed May 9, 2015. <http://www.threestooges.net/cast/actor/133>

"Weddings: Moore-Manahan." The *Sun* (NY), September 15, 1913.

# Epilogue:
# Spotlight Sisters

The last thirteen chapters were filled with women possessing tenacity, talent, and luck. They needed all three to get into the movies, but Vaudeville required all that plus more. There were no retakes: if their ability didn't back up their chutzpah, they'd be dumped faster than hooch during a raid. Sibling acts were legion: Fred and Adele Astaire, Buddy and Vilma Ebsen, The Five (yes, five) Marx Brothers, and The Nicholas Brothers being only a few. Sister acts were particularly endemic, and since I don't have enough ink to list them all, here are four whose circuit intersected with the silver screen.

## The Duncan Sisters

*Left: Rosetta and Vivian Duncan,* Picture Play, *June 1927. Right: Rosetta as Topsy and Vivian as Eva,* Photoplay, *May 1927. Photos courtesy the Media History Digital Library.*

These two California girls were one of the most recognizable duos in all of Vaudeville. The third and fourth of five children, Rosetta (born 1894) and Vivian (born 1897)[1] started out singing and dancing in a small-time Midwestern circuit. With the help of older sister Evelyn, they made it to New York and *Gus Edwards' Kiddie Revue*. Their little girl act, with Rosetta the capering clown to Vivian's dainty sausage-curled lass, earned them a small spot on Broadway in *Doing Our Part* (1917), with Ed Wynn and Frank Tinney. *She's a Good Fellow* (1918) and *Tip Top* (1920) quickly followed, where their "childish voices, close harmony and plenty of mischief"[2] laid the groundwork for what made them immortal: Topsy and Eva.

The musical comedy put Harriet Beecher Stowe's *Uncle Tom's Cabin* in the blender. The melodrama-free slurry that emerged made Topsy (Rosetta in blackface) and Eva (Vivian) the leads, singing (they wrote two songs themselves, one being the massive hit "Rememb'ring"), ad-libbing, and cavorting. The public couldn't get enough of them. They sailed through almost 200 performances in San Francisco, to nearly a year in Chicago, then New York, where they lit up Broadway for 159 performances. Critics were equally horrified and amused by the mutilation of Stowe's classic. The Duncans often interjected old bits or current events into the loosely-scripted show, assuring it was never the same twice. Critic and author Walter Kerr remembered Rosetta's signature curtain call, where she'd "grab at the house curtain as it started up . . . [u]p she went with the curtain, heels kicking like crazy."[3]

Their popularity led to a motion picture, *Topsy and Eva* (1927).[4] The production went way over budget and was fraught with problems, many due to Rosetta's difficult attitude. A revolving door of directors finally stopped on Del Lord and D.W. Griffith, but even their efforts couldn't save the complete flop. The whimsy and spontaneity that was the Duncans live was pitifully absent on film. They were cast not as Topsy and Eva but themselves in the early musical, *It's a Great Life* (1929), MGM's follow-up to *The Broadway Melody*. It failed to capture the former's magic and demand for the Duncans dropped; the act broke up in 1930 when Vivian married actor Nils Asther. (They had one daughter.)[5]

1931 brought bankruptcy, and between that and Vivian's 1932 divorce, both sisters were insolvent enough to bring Topsy and Eva out of mothballs. This time their draw was purely nostalgic, with most of their appearances leaning heavily on audience familiarity. They reprised the characters for the Warner Bros. Vitaphone short, *Surprise!* (1935), a radio sketch on *The Fleischmann Hour* with Rudy Vallee, and several TV guest spots. By 1942, they'd wrung everything they could out of the old act; their engagement at the Music Box was cancelled after only three weeks due to poor ticket sales.[6] One of their last performances together was on *The Liberace Show* in 1954, where Topsy and Eva sang "Rememb'ring." On December 4, 1959, Rosetta Duncan died of injuries sustained in a car accident. She was only 58.[7] Vivian continued to make the occasional solo appearance until her death from Alzheimer's disease on September 19, 1986. She was 89.[8]

## The Dolly Sisters

*The Dolly Sisters,* Picture Play, *March 1, 1916.*
Photo courtesy the Media History Digital Library.

Most movie buffs first learn of the Dolly Sisters via the 1945 film with Betty Grable and June Haver. Entertaining, but in true 1950s biopic fashion, almost completely inaccurate. They did get the most important thing right, however: the synchronized sisters' popularity.

Roszika and Janszieka (Yansci) Deutsch were born in Budapest, Hungary, in 1892.[9] The identical twins and their parents emigrated to the United States in 1905 and made their home in Far Rocka-way (Queens), New York. They were dancing by age eight and a Vaudeville act by 1909. A successful run at the Keith led to playing the Palace—the Holy Grail of Vaudeville—followed by the musical, *The Echo* (1910), where Ziegfeld discovered them and signed them to the *Ziegfeld Follies of 1911*.[10] Now named Rosie and Jenny, they continued to climb the ladder with Broadway's *A Winsome Widow* and *The Merry Countess* (both 1912), as well as the *Ziegfeld Follies of 1912*. They were striking, with their precise footwork and exotic looks topped by neat black bobs.

Rosie and Jenny briefly split in 1914 to focus on individual projects. Jenny had an act with her new husband, actor/dancer Harry Fox, and Rosie, married to songwriter Jean Schwartz since 1913, played Broadway. They dabbled separately in film but reunited to make *The Million Dollar Dollies* (1918) for Metro. The whisper-thin plot involving Maharajahs and jewels primarily existed to give a reason for opulent sets and lavish costumes by Lucile.[11]

The 1920s dawned bright for the deco Dollies. Both divorced by 1921, they were the toast of the town throughout the U.K. and Europe, where they introduced the Parisian *crème de la crème* to the Charleston and Black Bottom, and were courted by a glittering array of wealthy businessmen and royalty.[12] By 1924, they were back in the U.S. for *The Greenwich Village Follies*, their last Broadway appearance. They retired from performing in 1927, but not from the public eye; as the *New York Times* once said, "something was always happening to the Dolly girls."[13] They moved to the French Riviera and cleaned out the casino at Cannes, the $4 million funding Jenny's legendarily ostentatious diamond jewelry collection. In 1930, the prismatic Jenny won $280,000 in forty-eight hours of baccarat at Le Tourquet.[14]

Not everything revolved around money. Jenny adopted two little girls, Klari and Manzi, from a Hungarian orphanage in 1929. Harry Gordon Selfridge, of the U.K. department store dynasty, adored Jenny and spoiled her often with gifts; the two bonded over a shared passion for gambling. Rosie married Mortimer Davis Jr., son of Canadian tobacco baron Sir Mortimer Davis, but the union quickly soured and they divorced in 1931. A year later, New York City mayor Jimmy Walker officiated her wedding to Chicago department store scion Irving Netcher.[15]

A horrific 1933 car crash almost killed Jenny; it took her two years and seventeen operations[16] to improve enough to accompany Rosie and Irving back to Chicago. There she met attorney Bernard Vinissky and the two wed in 1935,[17] but it did little to assuage Jenny's depression, steadily worsening since the accident. On June 1, 1941, after phoning her aunt with complaints of feeling ill, Jenny Dolly hanged herself from a curtain rod in the apartment she shared with her daughters. (She and Vinissky had separated six months prior.) Jenny's aunt, worried by the phone call, rushed over and discovered her body.[18] Though Jenny left no note, her fragile mental state and financial troubles (she was forced to sell most of her jewelry) were certain catalysts. She was just 48.

Rosie retreated from the spotlight after her sister's death, living a quiet life of philanthropy toward the children of Hungary. After Netcher's death in 1953, Rosie sank into her own depression; she attempted suicide by overdose in 1962 but survived.[19] Rosie Dolly died of a heart attack on February 1, 1970. She was 77.[20]

## The Sisters G

The background of these two foreign beauties is as hazy as the nightclubs where they danced. Early publicity made them German and their father a colonel in the Prussian Guards, but this was mostly Hollywood claptrap. Eleanor and Karla Gutchrlein were likely born in the Netherlands in 1910. They were twins, but stories conflict whether they were identical.

Both their professional dance act and glossy black bobs were based on the Dolly Sisters. They performed for the elite in tony cities like London, Vienna, and Paris, where they joined Mistinguett

*The Sisters G,* Universal Weekly, *October 12, 1929. Photo courtesy the* Media History Digital Library.

at the Moulin Rouge, reportedly "the first German girls to dance in Paris after the war."[21] Allegedly discovered by *New York Times* war correspondent Lincoln Eyre, Carl Laemmle signed them in October 1929 for the upcoming "The King of Jazz Revue." The Gutchrleins were poised to conquer America in the Technicolor spectacular, renamed *King of Jazz* (1930) after its star, bandleader Paul Whiteman, but "[t]he good intentions of the Sisters G count[ed] for nothing" in a "mass of glittering over-production."[22]

Still, their Moderne moves got them noticed, and they filmed additional scenes for the German release of *King of Jazz*, brief numbers for a couple of other movies, and began a new stage show at the Fordham. *Variety* wasn't impressed and reserved praise only for costar Whitey Roberts, calling it "a long way from a Vaude act."[23] The last time we see the Sisters G is in God's *Gift to Women* (1931), with Frank Fay playing Don Juan to Laura La Plante, Joan Blondell, Louise Brooks, and Yola d'Avril. Eleanor and Karla's lavish musical number was axed due to changing tastes and all that remains are a few minutes of them in a nightclub scene.

So what became of the Gutchrleins? Did they return overseas and marry one of the wealthy aristocrats that wooed them back home? Did they stay in the U.S., and leave the glitterati behind, perfecting their English as stenographers or shop girls? The trail ended in 1932, with a brief mention of a Ziegfeld contract dispute,[24] then The Sisters G faded away, forever enigmatic and mysterious.

## The Brox Sisters

Hear the opening strains of "Singin' in the Rain" and you instantly conjure up Gene Kelly and his umbrella, but years before he splashed through the street it produced a very different image: three sweet songbirds named Brox.

The three youngest of John and Vinnie Goodrich Brock's six daughters[25] (their seventh child, a son named Nelson, died in infancy[26]), Eunice, Josephine, and Kathleen Brock first performed in a Canadian children's Vaudeville show after moving to Edmonton in the early 1900s. They spent the teens touring through Canada and the U.S., reaching New York and Irving Berlin's *Music Box*

*From L to R: Patricia, Bobbe, and Lorayne Brox,* What's On the Air, *February 1931. Photo courtesy the* Media History Digital Library.

*Revue* by 1921. Rechristened Lorayne, Bobbe (Dagmar for a short while), and Patricia Brox—the last name changed to fit better on a marquee, why the first names changed is anybody's guess—their tight harmonies and youthful *joie de vivre* were an instant hit. Berlin cast then in two more *Music Box* editions and wrote "Everybody Step" expressly for them.[27]

In 1926, they were cast in *The Cocoanuts,* The Marx Brothers' second Broadway production. "We were very young," recalled Bobbe. "Irving Berlin, who was our sponsor and guardian, told us one thing . . . 'now stay out of the way of those fellows.'"[28] The boys turned out to be madcap but mannerly. "[W]e never had more fun than working with the Marx Brothers, especially Groucho," said Lorayne.[29]

Next was the *Ziegfeld Follies of 1927,* with Eddie Cantor, a prolific spate of recording for Victor and Brunswick, and some of the first Vitaphone "talkie" shorts for Warner Bros. They were one of the bevy of stars that spangled MGM's *The Hollywood Revue of 1929,* along with Marie Dressler, Buster Keaton, Conrad Nagel, Cliff "Ukelele Ike" Edwards, John Gilbert, Norma Shearer, Laurel and Hardy, Jack Benny . . . the list was enormous. Along with Warner Bros.' *The Show of Shows* (1929), it showed a Hollywood teetering on the edge of revolution; within a year or two, many of the stars would be obsolete. *The Hollywood Revue of 1929* featured the Brox Sisters in the big Technicolor finale, introducing "Singin' in the Rain" for the first time on-screen as the entire cast, decked out in rain slickers, sang along.

The recently restored *Manhattan Serenade* (1929) teamed them with the woefully underused Nina Mae McKinney,[30] and the Paul Whiteman vehicle *King of Jazz* (1930) with The Rhythm Boys (featuring a young Bing Crosby). Songs in *Spring is Here* (1930) and the short *Hollywood on Parade* (1932) followed, as did radio's *The Fleischmann Hour*. "The trio is still the best of its kind," praised *Variety*, "moving in perfect unison and singing so quietly that it commands attention."[31]

All good things must come to an end, and the act dissolved in the 1930s as they married and settled down. They reunited one last time in 1929 for a radio tribute to Irving Berlin, one of their greatest supporters. Patricia died in 1988, Lorayne in 1993, and Bobbe, whose second marriage was to Sinatra songwriter Jimmy Van Heusen, died in 1999.[32]

1 Year: 1900; Census Place: Los Angeles Ward 7, Los Angeles, California; Roll: 90; Page: 4B; Enumeration District: 0076; FHL microfilm: 1240090. Ancestry.com. 1900 United States Federal Census [database on-line]. Provo, UT, USA: Ancestry.com Operations Inc, 2004.

2 Sullivan, John. "Topsy and Eva Play Vaudeville." *Uncle Tom's Cabin & American Culture*. Stephen Railton and the University of Virginia, 2000. Web. Accessed August 8, 2015. <http://utc.iath.virginia.edu/interpret/exhibits/sullivan/sullivan.html>

3 Kerr, Walter. "Musicals That Were Playful, Irresponsible, and Blissfully Irrelevant." *New York Times*, April 11, 1971.

4 "Topsy and Eva: The Movie." *Uncle Tom's Cabin & American Culture*. Stephen Railton and the University of Virginia. Web. Accessed August 8, 2015. <http://utc.iath.virginia.edu/onstage/films/duncmovhp.html>

5 "Vivian Duncan Weds Nils Asther of Films." *New York Times*, August 3, 1930.

6 "'Cry Havoc' Gets New Home." *New York Times*, November 23, 1942.

7 "Rosetta Duncan, Stage Star, Dies." *New York Times*, December 5, 1959.

8   Date: 1986-09-19. Ancestry.com. California, Death Index, 1940-1997 [database on-line]. Provo, UT, USA: Ancestry.com Operations Inc, 2000. State of California. California Death Index, 1940-1997. Sacramento, CA, USA: State of California Department of Health Services, Center for Health Statistics.

9   Frasier, David K. (2005). *Suicide in the Entertainment Industry: An Encyclopedia of 840 Twentieth Century Cases.* McFarland & Company, Inc.

10  "Jenny Dolly a Suicide by Hanging; She and Sister Won Dance Fame." *New York Times*, June 2, 1941.

11  Chapman, Gary. "The Million Dollar Dollies." *Jazz Age Club.* 2010. Web. Accessed September 12, 2015. <http://www.jazzageclub.com/film/the-million-dollar-dollies-1918/>

12  Cullen, Frank, Florence Hackman, Donald McNeilly (2004). *Vaudeville Old & New: An Encyclopedia of Variety Performances in America, Volume 1.* Psychology Press.

13  "Jenny Dolly a Suicide by Hanging," *New York Times*.

14  "Jenny Dolly Wins $280,000 In 2 Days' Baccarat in France." *New York Times*, June 13, 1930.

15  "Rozsika Dolly Weds Irving Netcher Here." *New York Times*, March 17, 1932.

16  "Jenny Dolly Is Back After Long Absence." *New York Times*, April 10, 1935.

17  "Jenny Dolly, Dancer, Wed." *New York Times*, June 30, 1935.

18  "Jenny Dolly a Suicide by Hanging," *New York Times*.

19  "Rosie Dolly Found Unconscious Here." *New York Times*, April 21, 1962.

20  "Rosie Dolly Netcher of the Dancing Sisters Dies." *New York Times*, February 2, 1970.

21  Warburton, Gertrude. "The Twin Sisters G." *Universal Weekly*, November 9, 1929.

22  "Over-Production Ruins Whiteman's Music in Film 'King of Jazz' at Roxy." *Variety*, May 7, 1930.

23  Earl. "New Acts." *Variety*, July 21, 1931.

24  "Lupe Understudy Files Claim Against Ziegfeld." *Variety*, June 14, 1932.

25  Item #91174, Census of the Northwest Provinces, 1906. *Library and Archives Canada.* Web. Accessed September 29, 2015. <http://www.bac-lac.gc.ca/eng>

26  "Find A Grave Index," database, FamilySearch (https://familysearch.org/ark:/61903/1:1:QVP3-MMXF : accessed 28 October 2015), Nelson Brock, 1891; Burial, Scranton, Greene, Iowa, United States of America, Scranton Township Cemetery; citing record ID 135276167, Find a Grave, http://www.findagrave.com.

27  "Music Box Revue Filled With Beauty." *New York Times*, December 2, 1924.

28  Chandler, Charlotte (1978). *Hello, I Must Be Going: Groucho and His Friends.* Doubleday & Company, Inc.

29  Ibid.

30  "Studio Sparks." *New York Times*, November 10, 1929.

31  "Broadway in Dutch As Par's Stage Show." *Variety*, May 21, 1930.

32  "Bobbe Brox, 98, Vocalist in a Family Trio." *New York Times*, May 15, 1999.

## Other Sources:

"A Duncan Sister Hurt." *New York Times*, December 2, 1959.

Aukerman, Cynthia. "Brox Sisters: from UC to Hollywood." *Winchester News-Gazette* (IN), January 22, 2007. Web. Accessed September 12, 2015. <http://www.winchesternewsgazette.com/articles/2007/01/23/news/news2.txt>

Chapman, Gary. "Mr. Selfridge and the Dolly Sisters." *Jazz Age Club.* 2010. Web. Accessed September 12, 2015. <http://www.jazzageclub.com/this-n-that/mr-selfridge-and-the-dolly-sisters-a-view/>

"Duncan Sisters Go Into Bankruptcy." *New York Times*, December 8, 1931.

"Duncans to End Act." *New York Times*, November 13, 1930.

"Rozsika Dolly." *IBDb – The Internet Broadway Database.* Web. Accessed August 21, 2015. <http://www.ibdb.com/Person/View/67346>

"'The Cocoanuts' Runs Off a Summer Edition." *New York Times*, June 11, 1926.

"Vivian Duncan Divorced." *New York Times*, November 11, 1932.

"Yansci Dolly." *IBDb – The Internet Broadway Database.* Web. Accessed August 21, 2015. <http://www.ibdb.com/Person/View/67347>

# Index

# About the Author

Jennifer Ann Redmond found her calling at age seven, when her essay won a countywide contest. Since then, her passion for writing, especially poetry, has been rivaled only by her love of the 1920s and 1930s. Silent and pre-Code (1929-1934) films are a particular favorite, and she counts Clara Bow, Louise Brooks, and Jean Harlow among her muses. Her work has been featured in *Classic Images*, *Vintage Life*, and *ZELDA* Magazine. Jennifer, a vintage girl in a modern world, currently resides in her childhood home on Long Island, New York.

Made in the USA
Middletown, DE
03 May 2016